DHARAMSALA

DHARAMSALA

TIBETAN REFUGE

◆

Jeremy Russell

◆

Foreword by
His Holiness the Dalai Lama

HEIAN INTERNATIONAL INC.

FREE TIBET

FOREWORD

Dharamsala has been my home for the greater part of my adult life since I left Tibet in 1959. I still remember well my first arrival here in the spring of 1960. We drove up by road from Pathankot station, through beautiful countryside, the lush green fields filled with trees and colourful flowers. After about an hour we caught our first glimpse of the gleaming white mountains of the Dhauladhar range towering in the distance. These peaks were also the first sight to greet my eyes when I awoke for the first time in my new home the following morning, and of course their presence remains the dominating feature of the landscape.

Dharamsala was where I was finally able to settle down after several years' pressure trying to deal with the Chinese occupation of my homeland, followed by the turmoil of my escape to India. Those early days were marked by a new kind of freedom, for although there was a lot of work to do ensuring the welfare of our ever increasing community of refugees, I finally had time and leisure to give more attention to my studies and my spiritual practice. In addition, I was physically freer and enjoyed walking and trekking into the nearby woods and hills. Dharamsala then was very much an abandoned British hill station, a quiet and sleepy backwater of the Punjab, not the bustling Himachali town that it is today. My mother shared those early years with me and it was here that she happily spent her final days.

During our stay here, we Tibetans have been able to construct several institutions that have served not only to enable us to preserve our identity and traditions, but also to share them with others. I believe that our schools and religious establishments, our government offices, the Institute for Performing Arts, the Library of Tibetan Works and Archives, the Tibetan Medical and Astrological Institute, the Norbulingka Institute and so forth vividly display Tibetans' resourcefulness and the richness and value of our ancient culture. This is one of the paradoxical benefits of our time in exile, for when Tibet was free few people from the outside world had access to it and our way of life was often shrouded in mystery and misunderstood.

One of the great personal pleasures of moving to my present residence in 1968 was that it gave me the opportunity to work in my garden, where I am able to plant trees and tend flowers with my own hands. However, this pleasure is also related to one of my few disappointments with life here. For much of the year, the summer and autumn especially, we enjoy a comfortable, pleasant climate, but this all changes in the humidity of monsoon. Dharamsala suffers from over-abundant rainfall, which, besides creating havoc in the garden, is causing increasingly severe damage to the local hillsides and the environment in general. It is then in particular that I miss the drier weather of Tibet.

Apart from this small reservation, I look back on my years so far in Dharamsala as happy ones. Having made me and my people warmly welcome since our first arrival, the people of Dharamsala have continued to show us remarkable kindness and affection over the years. Whatever the future may hold, and whenever our dreams of returning freely to our homeland are fulfilled, we will never forget our time in this delightful place that has served us as true refuge.

January 28, 1999

Introduction

✢

Dharamsala denotes a place of shelter for pilgrims, usually a hostel attached to one of the myriad temples that dot the Indian landscape. It is an apt name for the small hill town that is the headquarters of Kangra District in the north Indian state of Himachal Pradesh—for Dharamsala has functioned as a shelter of sorts right from the start and continues to do so today.

Following the British seizure of the Kangra fort and the annexation of Kangra district, Dharamsala was established as a hill station. It was host to sick soldiers and administrative officers and British wives and children escaping the heat of the plains in summer.

In 1947, many people left Dharamsala and moved to the newly created Pakistan, a relatively short journey away. At the same time, many travelled in the opposite direction, leaving their homes in Rawalpindi, Lahore and Peshawar, and arrived in Dharamsala. Many of them settled there and rebuilt their lives.

Barely thirteen years later, in 1960, His Holiness the Dalai Lama of Tibet was invited to take up temporary residence in Dharamsala, after his dramatic flight from his country following the Chinese communist takeover. He was accompanied by his family, his teachers and close advisors; eventually, a substantial lay and monastic Tibetan community followed him. He set up an administration of this new refugee community in Dharamsala that is, in effect, a government-in-exile.

At the beginning of the twenty-first century, Dharamsala is busy and thriving once more. Its population has expanded tremendously since the sleepy days before the Tibetans came, and building, both planned and unplanned, has proceeded apace. Besides becoming one of the most important towns of Himachal Pradesh, Dharamsala has become a major tourist destination. People flock not only from all over India, but from every corner of the globe to this quiet refuge. And yet, true to its historically cosmopolitan character, remarkable telecommunication facilities and a proliferation of Internet cafés, this shelter in the hills is no longer remote but in constant touch with the world at large.

Historical Background

✠

Dharamsala looks out over the beautiful Kangra valley, a region rich in ancient history. The kings of Kangra belonged to one of the oldest traceable genealogical lines in India. In the distant past the kingdom of Trigarta, and later the kingdom of Jalandhara, extended from the Dhauladhar mountains of the outer Himalayan range down to the plains. It was in this vicinity that Alexander the Great came to a final halt on the banks of the Beas river which runs from above Manali down through the Kangra valley until it reaches the plains. Aryan and Indian Pali inscriptions on a pair of boulders below Khanyara near Dharamsala dating to the end of the 1st century BCE (Before the Common Era or Before the Christian Era) suggest that there was a Buddhist monastery, the Krishna-yasasa Arama, nearby. Other archaeological evidence—Buddhist statues and so forth—suggest that the kingdom of Jalandhara was a centre of Hindu/Buddhist tantricism in the 7th century, when Buddhism was carried to Tibet. Chetru below Dharamsala is something of an archaeological mystery. Some assert that it has associations with the Pandava brothers, but there is also a suggestion that Chetru comes from the word *chaitya* or stupa, which may have stood at the confluence of two rivers. Further afield, the unique rock-cut temples at Masroor dedicated to Shiva, and the delightful temple compound at Baijnath are more than one thousand years old.

When the Muslim army of Mahmud of Ghazni entered India, it laid siege to the Kangra fort in 1009 CE and plundered the Kangra temple for its wealth. The temple at Jwalamukhi, where the deity is represented by flames emerging naturally from the ground, was admired by the Mughal emperor Akbar, who is alleged to have offered the gilded roof. Yet, today, visitors will be hard-pressed to find any sign that Muslims were ever there, their homes, places of worship and burial grounds seemingly forgotten.

Otherwise, what distinguishes Dharamsala from an ancient town like Kangra is not only its relative youth, but the fact that it has always been and

Pages 12-13: The cool and peace of the wooded hills initially attracted the British to Dharamsala.

Pages 14-15: Dharamsala with the Dauladhar mountain range towering behind it.

Pages 16-17: Monks of Namgyal monastery constructing a sand mandala.

remains so cosmopolitan. The British founded it and attracted people to work for them. This polity included Sikhs and other Punjabis, people from Jammu and Gurkhas from Nepal. They came to live side by side with the indigenous people of the land, the Kangri people of the valley and the nomadic Gaddi tribes. Legend has it that four or five hundred years ago, the Gaddis migrated from Rajasthan, having lost their land there. They came to inhabit this region and the consequent Gaddi realm encompassed the Dhauladhar range from Kullu up to Chamba. These nomadic Hindu shepherds, as distinct from the Muslim Gujjar cattleherds elsewhere in Himachal Pradesh, take their flocks of sheep and goats over the high passes to seek mountain pastures in summer and the monsoon, but spend winter in the Kangra valley, where many own houses and land.

Pages 18-19: The Gaddi shepherds, indigenous to the hills around Dharamsala, lead their flocks over the high passes to richer pastures in summer and return to the Kangra valley in winter.

The British Era

✝

Dharamsala was founded by the British who occupied the Kangra fort in 1846 and annexed the kingdom of Kangra. They then sought a cooler elevated position, from which they could overlook the Kangra valley, to garrison their forces. Thus, they established what is now the cantonment on the spur of the hills that has come to be known as Dharamsala. The army camp continues to have a commanding view of the valley.

Earlier the kings of Kangra had also occupied these hills for much the same reasons. Accounts of the origin of the name Dharamsala vary—one tells that Dharam Chand, a king, built some kind of a fort on Dharamkot hill, another secure vantage point. He also apparently erected a *dharamsala*, a place for people to rest, while waiting for an audience with him.

In due course, with the British army settled on the ridge, civilian residences came up in the woods above. The initial temporary camp at Dharamsala was upgraded into a cantonment in 1849. At the same time, the local Divisional Commissioner, John Lawrence, later Commissioner for the Punjab and Viceroy, built one of the first civilian houses. Eventually the cantonment attracted to it settlements which later became the villages of McLeod Ganj and Forsyth Ganj, where people who served the army as cooks, cleaners, tailors, and so forth, lived. The building of the Church of St. John in the Wilderness in 1852 is indicative of how settled the community became in a relatively short time. Villas occupied by officials such as the Deputy Commissioner and the Forest Officer came up in the forest above McLeod Ganj. It was as if the hillside had been laid out in order of social status. The civilian officers had villas up on the hill; the military were a little further down and the offices of the civil administration were below them.

One of Dharamsala's most enduring landmarks is Mr Nowrojee's shop which dates back to about 1860. The fact that this thriving Parsee businessman from Lahore saw fit to establish a branch in the hills is evidence that there was a sufficiently large community to be served by such an enterprising provisioner.

Lord Elgin of Kincardine was Viceroy of India from 1860 to 1863. He developed a particular fondness for Dharamsala and it was probably this affection that gave rise to the legend that Dharamsala was to become the summer capital of British India. In any event he did not live to fulfill this wish, for he died in Dharamsala in 1863. His widow endowed an elaborate memorial to him that stands beyond the head of the church, and a pair of stained-glass windows, attributed to Edwin Byrne-Jones (1833-1898), English painter, designer and illustrator who was a member of the pre-Raphaelite movement.

The memorial to Lord Elgin, Viceroy of India, was erected by his widow after he died in Dharamsala. It stands beyond the head of the church.

Facing page: Mrs Nowrojee looks out from the entrance to the shop owned by her husband's family for nearly a century and a half.

The inscription reads: Hari Om Mani Padme Hum— *Hail to the Jewel in the Lotus.*

Facing page: Woman prays on lingor *path around the palace of His Holiness the Dalai Lama.*

The British community continued to thrive, attracting all kinds of people including sick soldiers and wives of officers and missionaries, who treated Dharamsala as a place of rest. Consequently, it developed into a classic hill station, which with Dalhousie, would have served Lahore as much as Delhi and the rest of the huge pre-partition Punjab. Even today, if you walk westwards out of McLeod Ganj, you can imagine the *pukka sahibs* riding the narrow roads and myriad cobbled paths to the church on Sundays and perhaps on to Mr Nowrojee's shop to pick up something to while away the afternoon.

Having come up as a British settlement, Dharamsala took a major blow on April 4, 1905, when a huge earthquake struck it early in the morning with devastating force. Eyewitness accounts relate that all the buildings in the Kangra area were either demolished or rendered uninhabitable. The church was one of the very few buildings to survive, but most of the residential areas of Kangra and Dharamsala had to be rebuilt. In this process, a major relocation took place, giving rise to the upper, middle and lower areas of the town. With the reconstruction, the courts, police station and lock-up, as well as offices of the various administrative departments were re-established in lower Dharamsala, where they still stand today. The market was reconstructed at what is now Kotwali Bazaar. Inevitably, the villas and bungalows of the hill station proper came up again in the forests above McLeod Ganj and Forsyth Ganj, for only there at 6000 feet above sea level was there any real refuge from the summer heat.

Life in Dharamsala saw gradual improvements such as the construction of the hydroelectric powerhouse at Jogindernagar, which brought electricity to the hill station in the late 1920s, and the introduction of the Kangra Valley narrow-gauge railway. At the same time, the Nowrojees introduced the first two cars that ran up to Dharamsala from the railhead at Pathankot. Even now, older residents remember how Dharamsala used to be supplied from Pathankot by bullock and camel cart.

With Indian independence approaching in 1947, many of the British planned to stay on. However, the horrors that accompanied the unfortunate partition of the country put paid to their dreams. Dharamsala, the tranquil and slightly remote hill station, suddenly found itself relatively close to the newly wrought border. One of the effects was a substantial migration of people to Pakistan. Some people say that 70 per cent of the people in Kotwali Bazaar left in the late summer of 1947. In turn many families arrived from Peshawar, Rawalpindi, Lahore and those regions of Punjab and the North West Frontier that had ended up as Pakistan. With the dreadful carnage that took place in this great upheaval, many Britishers, who had thought they would make a go of it in the *new* India, took fright, fled and never returned. The upper reaches of Dharamsala, where the British and European population used to live, was largely abandoned. The bungalows and villas were left behind in the care of Mr Nowrojee, who, amongst so many other things, was the local estate agent.

Over the next twelve or thirteen years, upper Dharamsala became quite dilapidated. In 1960, the newly exiled Dalai Lama was invited to settle in Dharamsala rather than in Mussoorie, where he had been provided initial sanctuary. It seems that he and the refugees following him received an especially sympathetic reception from the population of Dharamsala, many of whom had not long before been refugees themselves. The latter knew what it was like to lose the land they had grown up in and to have to rebuild their lives elsewhere. With the arrival of the Dalai Lama and the Tibetans who gathered around him, Dharamsala gained a new lease of life.

What remains today of the British era are a few bungalows and villas which have since been occupied by Tibetans and have acquired other associations. Swarg Ashram, for example, the house where the Dalai Lama first lived in Dharamsala, is now the Mountaineering Institute. The house a

The bell of the Church of St. John in the Wilderness was broken in the earthquake in 1905. Though a new bell was cast in London and carried to India, it was never raised to the tower again.

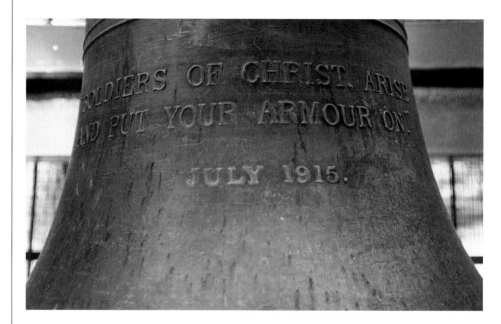

little further up the hill where his junior tutor, Trijang Rinpoche, first lived, now functions as the Tushita Meditation Centre. Dharamsala cantonment, like other cantonments the length and breadth of India, is home to regiments of the Indian army. Due to its mild climate and pleasant environment, Dharamsala continues to be regarded as an enviable posting by army officials.

Mr Nowrojee's shop, which provided for the British community from 1860 until 1947, still does thriving business and is filled with mementos of those bygone times. It offers priceless candy jars, rare advertising cards, placards, fixtures and fittings dating from a period of greater prosperity and which are older than most of the people visiting the shop. The Nowrojees were innovators in many ways: apart from being provision merchants and newsagents, they ran an aerated water plant, provided the only local taxi service and functioned as auctioneers and estate agents. The present Mr Nowrojee, who is now in his eighties, is one of the few people to have witnessed the entire ebb and flow of Dharamsala's history.

The Church of St. John in the Wilderness

✢

Known as the 'army church', the Church of St. John in the Wilderness was built in 1852 to meet the needs of the British soldiers posted at Dharamsala. Standing alone amidst the towering deodar (Himalayan cedar) trees, it might be mistaken for a quiet kirk (church) somewhere in Scotland. This sturdy stone building, well constructed of hand-dressed local granite, withstood the 1905 earthquake, although pieces of the broken front scattered here and there are evidence that it suffered significant damage. There used to be a steeple, and presumably a bell, which apparently fell at that time. A new bell was cast in London, surprisingly in 1915 when Europe was embroiled in war. And, although we can imagine its long and careful journey by sea, probably to Bombay, then by rail to Pathankot and from there to the church by bullock cart, it was never raised into the tower again, but remained hung from beams resting between supporting walls in the garden outside. This support was rebuilt in 1995 and inaugurated by the Duke of Gloucester who was fortuitously visiting Dharamsala at the time. When thieves attempted to steal this bell in the spring of 1998, they fortunately dropped it, relatively unharmed, a couple of hundred yards up the road.

In the church itself there are plaques mostly commemorating military men who have died, but rarely in action. There is a famous one for the man who died in a fight with a bear and another above the organ, put up by a girl for her poor young fiancée who died on the eve of their wedding. In the graveyard are buried people who died in Dharamsala, presumably of ailments like dysentery and diarrhoea that we would not expect to be fatal these days. A century and a half ago, there were no antibiotics and probably an insufficient supply of clean water. There are many graves of small children. It is also touching how many of the gravestones were put up by fellow officers and soldiers as a mark of affection and esteem.

The Arrival of the Tibetans

✢

With the coming of the Tibetans, upper Dharamsala began to stir once more. For the first decade—throughout the sixties—life must have been very difficult for the refugees. Most of them worked at building roads and lived in makeshift camps. They were traumatised—having fled their homes and having lost their country to the invading Chinese. They lived in great expectation that they would return soon, that the dispute with China would be settled swiftly. In retrospect, those years were a transitional period

A new arrival in Dharamsala awaits an audience with the Dalai Lama.

Mother of Ngawarg Gyaltzen, a musicologist trained in Dharamsala and USA, and who has been imprisoned by the Chinese for 18 years in Tibet.

Families just arrived from Tibet await their fate.

Father and daughter are united after many years when he is able to leave Tibet at last.

as the exiled Tibetan community came to terms with what had happened. Even in the early seventies most Tibetans were still living in makeshift houses put together from fruit and vegetable boxes with flattened oil tins for roofing.

However, the Dalai Lama lost no time in assembling a secretariat which would function both as a government-in-exile and administer the refugee community. He received a great deal of backing and encouragement from the then Indian Prime Minister Jawaharlal Nehru. Many Tibetans in those early years expected that they would receive support to fight the Chinese and somehow reclaim their country. However, what Nehru counselled the Dalai Lama to do if he wished to save his culture and his nation, was to ensure the education of Tibetan children. He was convinced that that was the way to secure Tibet's future.

Thekchen Chöling—the Tsuglagkhang and the Dalai Lama's Palace

✟

In the early years of the Tibetan settlement in Dharamsala, the Dalai Lama was accommodated in a house known as Swarg Ashram, which sits on extensive grounds on the road climbing into the woods above McLeod Ganj.

At that time his two tutors also occupied houses on the same hill: Trijang Rinpoche lived in the house which is now the Tushita Meditation Centre and the senior tutor, Ling Rinpoche, lived a little higher up in Chopra House. This is where the Tibetan administration was initially centred.

In the course of time, various religious bodies were attracted to His Holiness's presence. For example, the Namgyal Monastery, the Dalai Lama's personal monastery, which had been temporarily established in Dalhousie in the mid 60s, moved to Dharamsala. In the early years of exile few Tibetans thought that they were going to be in exile for a long time. Initially they made little effort to re-establish their institutions such as temples and others. But after nearly ten years, there was an urge to build the present Tsuglagkhang or main temple at Thekchen Chöling on the crest of the ridge which McLeod Ganj bestrides.

However, mindful of the refugee community's limited budget, the Dalai Lama made it clear that the need was not to build a lavish temple as they would have done in Tibet. What was required was a simple, functional building which would allow people to gather to observe their religious ceremonies and practices. This is why the temple is a plain and square concrete structure. Nevertheless, the original building has continued to be extended and improved upon.

On entering the temple, as everyone is welcome to do even when there are religious functions taking place, the visitor's first encounter is with a large statue of Buddha Shakyamuni, the historical Buddha. Seated in saffron robes in a posture of meditation, his right hand touches the ground, calling

When mothers are at work, their babies stay here.

Life in exile offers some freedom from fear.

Pages 28-29: His Holiness the Fourteenth Dalai Lama—Dharamsala's most revered resident.

Pages 30-31: Long-life ceremony for the Dalai Lama in the Tsnglagkhang—the main temple.

the earth to witness his awakening to enlightenment. His left hand rests in his lap, holding the alms bowl of a monk. This statue of the Buddha is the major focus of the temple. As people enter, they pay their respects, often by bowing down three times and touching their heads to the ground in prostration, as a mark of admiration and aspiration of attaining the state of enlightenment themselves.

On either side of the statue are cupboards from floor to ceiling, containing the volumes of the two major collections of Tibetan Buddhist scriptures: the *Kangyur*—the translated words of the Buddha and the *Tengyur*—the collection of translated commentaries of later Buddhist teachers. These books are long and narrow, emulating the original palm-leaf manuscripts of ancient India. They are placed lengthways in the cabinet so that only the ornate tags bearing their titles can be seen.

On the eastern wall, next to the door, hangs a large painting depicting the three religious kings of Tibet: Songtsen Gampo (born 605 CE), Trisong Detsen (born 742 CE) and Ralpachen (died 848 CE), who are honoured for having initiated the introduction of Buddhism into Tibet. During the reign of

Pages 32-33: His Holiness the Dalai Lama participates in prayers in the Tsnglagkhang. Behind him is the statue of Shakyamuni, the historical Buddha. The statue is flanked by cupboards containing the scriptures. To the right of the Dalai Lama are statues of Padmasambhava or Guru Rimpoche and a thousand armed Avalokiteshvara.

King Songtsen Gampo, Tibet had become a major military power in Asia, its influence extending well into western China, up to Mongolia, down to the banks of the Ganges, and even westwards towards Swat in what is now Pakistan. It is almost as if Songtsen Gampo realised that the country had reached its peak in one aspect of its development and, in order to lead the nation in a new direction, had set about introducing Buddhist culture, primarily from India.

This entailed developing a written language. Taking a Sanskrit model, a written language and grammar were composed by one of the king's ministers, Thonmi Sambhota, who had been sent to Kashmir for this purpose. A huge project was then begun to translate the existing Sanskrit literature into Tibetan and literally create a body of literature which emulated and simulated Indian Buddhist culture. This enterprise continued under the auspices of the other two religious kings.

Amongst King Songtsen Gampo's several wives, Princess Brikuti from Nepal and Princess Wengchen from China encouraged his awareness of Buddhism. Under their influence the Lhasa Tsuglagkhang or Jokhang and

The Dalai Lama in the audience chambers of his palace in Dharamsala.

Ramoche temples were constructed. During the reign of King Trisong Detsen a century later, Buddhism was formally declared the state religion and Tibet's first Buddhist institutions were established. The great Indian abbot Shantarakshita ordained the first seven Tibetan monks and tried to found a monastery. But, so the story goes, Tibet's local spirits were opposed to his activities, and whatever was built during the day was demolished at night.

Shantarakshita informed the king that he did not have sufficient influence to achieve what was required and recommended that he invite the great charismatic adept, Padmasambhava, the Lotus Born Guru, from India, which Trisong Detsen duly did. Padmasambhava visited Tibet, pacified the interfering forces, and, with Shantarakshita, established the great monastery of Samye (767 CE) and many other religious establishments. Both these important figures are depicted in the painting, in the space above and behind the three kings.

Padmasambhava or Guru Rinpoche, the Precious Guru as he is popularly known, is also portrayed in the large fierce-looking statue seated in the alcove on the western side of the temple. He is regarded by many Tibetans with a respect and gratitude second only to that accorded the historical Buddha, because he actually established Buddhism in Tibet.

To the left of the statue of Padmasambhava is a large standing statue with eleven heads and a thousand arms, each of which has an eye in the palm of the hand. This is a representation of Avalokitesvara or Chenresig—the Bodhisattva of compassion, who is as close as is possible to being the patron deity of Tibet. It is his six-syllable mantra, *Om Manipadme Hung,* which is on the lips of so many Tibetans as they go about their lives. Moreover, the Dalai Lamas are traditionally regarded as human emanations of Avalokitesvara, so there is clearly a very strong link between this deity and Tibet.

At the feet of the Avalokitesvara statue there is a small glass-fronted cabinet containing some broken stone heads which belonged to a very

Pages 36-37: Monks of Namgyal Monastery blow long horns while members of the Tibetan Government-in-Exile look on during the New Year rooftop ceremonies.

Namgyal monks perform a ceremony in the Kalachakra Temple.

similar statue that used to stand in the Jokhang in Lhasa. It was destroyed in 1967 during the cultural revolution and these fragments were salvaged and brought to India. They were presented to the Dalai Lama, who placed them here.

To the left of the Avalokitesvara is a small statue of Dipankara Atisha, the great Indian Buddhist teacher from the monastery of Vikramashila, who was invited to Tibet in 1042. By this time the initial wave of Buddhist culture had become somewhat diffused and confused. Dipankara Atisha brought a new clarity to Tibetan Buddhism, emphasising the need for the monastic community to be pure. He also established the renowned genre of Buddhist literature that is known as the *Stages of the Path of Enlightenment*. In this he laid out, in an easily comprehensible form, the stages of spiritual practice from the simplest aspiration for freedom from anguished rebirth to liberation, to final enlightenment for the sake of all sentient beings.

Placed before this set of statues are offerings of bowls of clean water and butter lamps, typical of Tibetan Buddhist temples. The golden lamps before the Avalokitesvara and Padmasambhava statues are offered particularly when people wish to pray for the sick and the recently dead.

Hanging on the walls of the temple are *thangkas,* the scroll paintings which often depict stories from the Buddha's life or illustrate meditational, or long-life, tutelary deities. These are painted on cloth and mounted on lavish silk brocade. Many Tibetans lived a nomadic existence and these paintings could be rolled up and carried with them when they set off for the next pasture.

Behind the temple are the kitchens where enormous cauldrons—five or six feet across—are heated over wood fires to boil huge amounts of tea when

there are large gatherings in the temple. There are occasions when two or three thousand monks and nuns and, perhaps, as many lay people assemble to listen to the Dalai Lama's public teachings as part of the Great Prayer Festival in spring.

Besides being a location for public teaching, the temple is a place where people come to offer personal prayers. They also come to make offerings before the Dalai Lama's throne, a throne that is erected out of respect for religious teaching. In fact, when the Dalai Lama himself comes to sit on that throne in order to teach, he first bows before it. This is a throne on which only he can sit and, as such, paying respect to the throne is like paying respect to him. The temple is also a site for the public and the monastic communities of the locality to gather to say prayers, which they do at various times throughout the year. Sometimes they gather for week-long sessions during which they recite 100,000 prayers or offerings and a great number of mantras. Outside, individuals can often be seen performing prostrations and they too may have a target of 100,000.

His Holiness the Dalai Lama presides over the rooftop ceremonies at the Tibetan New Year, wherein offerings are made to Palden Lhamo (Sri Devi).

The Namgyal Monastery

Adjacent to the main temple are the buildings of the Namgyal Monastery, which has a special function in the Tibetan Buddhist structure because of its long association with the Dalai Lamas. This began with the third Dalai Lama, Sonam Gyatso, when he was accepted as spiritual mentor of the Mongol chieftain Gushri Khan, from whom he received the title 'Dalai Lama' in tribute to his oceanic qualities. He gathered some monks together to say

The New Temple in the Namgyal Monastery. Thangkas *and deities being consecrated during Buddha's descent from Tushita (heavenly realms).*

regular prayers for the long life of Gushri Khan and this group seems eventually to have evolved into the Namgyal Monastery.

When the Fifth Dalai Lama became the overall ruler of a united Tibet and established himself in the Potala Palace, which he had built on the Red Hill in Lhasa, the Namgyal Monastery was accommodated in the red West Wing. The monastery came to have great significance in the Ganden Podrang government founded by the Fifth Dalai Lama. This unique spiritual and temporal form of government consisted of both monastic and lay officials, 175 of each, and to echo these numbers, there were 175 monks in the Namgyal Monastery.

Tibetan women churning salt, butter and tea leaves in a traditional domo.

Their function was to perform rituals and prayers for the benefit of Tibet and to support the Dalai Lama in his religious activities. To this day the Dalai Lama's personal attendants are drawn from amongst the monks of the Namgyal Monastery. They support him when he is expounding Buddhist teachings and performing ceremonies such as tantric initiations. When he grants the Kalachakra initiation, which he gives to large groups of people, he is supported by a team of about 18 monks from the Namgyal Monastery. They are skilled in the arts of creating sand *mandalas*, performing the dances, manufacturing the requisite ritual cakes, and so forth.

Offerings of candles for the Long Life puja of the Dalai Lama.

Of the 175 monks belonging to the monastery in Tibet, about 30 managed to escape into exile. Of these, half survived and were able to train a new body of monks when the monastery was re-established in Dharamsala. They have passed on nearly all the ritual traditions of the Namgyal Monastery. However, the Dalai Lama is particularly concerned that there should no longer be such a proliferation of monasteries whose only function is to perform rituals, as there was sometimes in Tibet. He feels it is important that monks should have sufficient education to understand what they are doing in the rituals and to understand the context in which they function. The monks of Namgyal Monastery, like the monks of Nechung Monastery, have added to their curriculum of ritual studies, studies of Buddhist philosophy and the practice of debate, in addition to a certain amount of modern education. They now have a much broader command of their ancient Buddhist culture than perhaps their predecessors would have had in Tibet.

For many years, the Namgyal Monastery used the Tsuglagkhang temple as the site for many of the rituals which they perform in a cycle, a calendar of events throughout the year. Ultimately a need emerged for another location, so they constructed alongside the main temple what has come to be known as the Kalachakra temple. This is mainly because the paintings on its walls were dominated by depictions of the Kalachakra *mandala*. Now the monastery is able to continue their cycle of practices, even when the main temple is in use for other purposes.

The paintings on the three walls at the head of the temple illustrate the Namgyal Monastery's spiritual inheritance. On either side are the body and mind *mandalas* of the meditational deity Kalachakra, representing his celestial mansion and entourage of meditational deities.

The paintings inside this temple are particularly fine examples of Tibetan Buddhist artwork. The artists here have emulated the technique used for painting *thangkas*. A canvas was attached to the wall and teams of painters worked for 18 months on scaffolding to complete the project.

Thekchen Chöling is the focus of the Tibetan New Year celebrations, which generally take place in February or March. First, there are ceremonies to dispose of the symbols of the old year and any residual negativity to be able to begin the new year afresh. The new year dawns with a ceremony on the temple roof presided over by the Dalai Lama. This consists of solemn prayers to Palden Lhamo (Sri Devi), one of the state guardians of Tibet. Two weeks later, on the fifteenth of the first Tibetan month, the full moon day, the traditional Great Prayer Festival begins with the Dalai Lama reading one of the stories of the births of the Buddha prior to his life as the historical Buddha. This is followed by what has come to be known as the Spring Teachings—two weeks in which the Dalai Lama gives religious discourses to the public. This used to take place in the temple itself with the Dalai Lama sitting on the throne, surrounded by monks and nuns, and the lay people behind them, spilling out on to the verandahs and walkways. In the

Even Namgyal Monastery thinks different with an Apple Mackintosh!

mid-nineties, the Dalai Lama decided that it is more convenient for everyone to gather in the temple garden.

At the far end from the temple in the garden is the gate to the Dalai Lama's personal residential compound. The first set of buildings beyond the gate contain his private office, audience chambers, and so forth. His personal residence stands in the garden, just over the peak of the hill. The audience chambers are where he meets individuals for personal or private interviews and where he receives large groups who come to take his blessings. He makes a point of meeting everybody who reaches Dharamsala from Tibet.

Institute of Buddhist Dialectics

Behind and below the temple is the Institute of Buddhist Dialectics, an ecumenical school of monks who train in the tradition of dialectics followed in the great monastic institutions of Tibet. Formal debate or dialectics is a means by which logic can be applied to the meaning of the scriptures, ensuring that a correct and affirmed understanding can be maintained. Traditionally monks memorise the text they are studying—often the translation of an Indian Buddhist text. After that they receive an oral explanation of the text and then debate their understanding with their fellow students.

Customarily, one monk stands and, with elaborate gestures, poses a challenging question to his colleague seated on the ground who, in turn, seeks to answer. This is not merely an intellectual, but also a highly physical exercise involving the clapping of hands, the stamping of feet and the swinging of rosaries, which symbolise driving out misunderstandings and awakening

beings from the sleep of ignorance. The process stimulates a sharpness of intellect and a very deep and thorough understanding of the material studied. Most days, during the late afternoon, visitors to Thekchen Chöling may find monks from the Institute of Buddhist Dialectics or from the Namgyal Monastery in the temple garden practising this skill. It is a great spectacle.

The Mani Path

Running around the crest of the ridge, on which the temple and the Dalai Lama's residence stand, is a path popularly known as the Lingkhor, the circumambulatory path or the Mani Path. Like many circumambulatory routes in Tibet, it is lined by heaps of stones marked with the six-syllable mantra *Om Manipadme Hung*. People take a turn around the hill particularly during the early morning and evening, combining the benefits of a brisk walk with the spiritual potential of paying respect to religious objects. At a couple of places next to the path you will come across a tent sheltering a man carving *mani* stones, which the devout buy from him to place on one of the cairns. Below the path, an old people's home for retired members of the Tibetan administration has recently been established.

Shrines of the three protective deities of Tibet. The prayer flags behind hang over the Lingkhor or the Mani Path (the circumambulatory path).

Facing page: An early morning devotee turns one of the giant prayer wheels as he circumambulates the Mani Path.

At the southernmost point the path opens out into a great yard where, particularly on Wednesdays when the Dalai Lama is out of town, Tibetans offer incense and hoist prayer flags to Tibet's protective deities to ensure his welfare. These pieces of coloured cloth have been imprinted with prayers or sections of scripture carved on wood blocks, whose spirit is then carried over the land by the wind.

Gangchen Kyishong: The Tibetan Government-in-Exile

Further down the hill is the compound known as Gangchen Kyishong, the seat of the Tibetan government-in-exile. This is where the Assembly of Tibetan People's Deputies, the elected parliament-in-exile oversees the running of the various departments of the administration including the Departments of Religion and Culture, Home, Education, Health, Finance, Information and International Relations. These various departments have a dual function of contributing to the struggle for freedom in Tibet, besides administering to the needs of the Tibetan refugee community.

The Parliament-in-Exile during a session. The parliament supervises the running of the various departments of administration.

Facing page: An accomplished nun often consulted for divination about the future and other issues.

The Tibetan Library

One of the earliest buildings in Gangchen Kyishong is the Library of Tibetan Works and Archives. Established in 1971, it is the cultural repository of the community-in-exile. When the Dalai Lama left Tibet in 1959, many of the people who followed him carried little more than what they stood up in. However, during the ensuing decade, people continued to leave Tibet and, recognising the threat that the Chinese presence in Tibet posed to Tibetan culture, they brought statues, paintings and books with them, many of them salvaged from destroyed monasteries and temples. These they would bring to Dharamsala to offer to the Dalai Lama. By the end of the sixties, the Dalai Lama recognised the need for an institution to preserve this unique collection of Tibetan artefacts and founded the Library of Tibetan Works and Archives in 1971.

When it was built, the Tibetan Library, as it is fondly known, was the only Tibetan-style building in Dharamsala, which made it something of a cultural asset by itself. It was modelled on an aristocratic house which used to stand in Lhasa and has such typical features as the broad base with whitewashed walls which taper inwards as the building rises. The deep windows have the broad black border known as a beard; the protruding sill above, and a red frieze which runs around the top of the walls. But what immediately catches the eye is the highly decorative verandah with its brightly painted pillars and capitals in front of the grand red doors with their tassled brass knobs.

Books occupy the entire ground floor. These include 70,000 Tibetan books and documents brought out of Tibet and about 10,000 books in English and foreign languages dealing with Buddhism and Tibet-related affairs.

Tibetan literature has its origins in the great translating enterprise which began in the 7th and 8th centuries. It continued through to the 13th century in an ongoing process of refinement and editing until the scriptures had been gathered in two main collections: the *Kangyur,* or translations of the actual words of the Buddha, and the *Tengyur,* the supplementary commentaries of later Buddhist teachers. When they embarked on this great project, Tibetans took great pains to emulate Indian literature in every respect. They even followed the physical pattern of the books, writing them on long strips of paper which resembled the palm leaves of ancient Indian scriptures. In the centre of these pages two circles would be drawn indicating the position where a cord was threaded through the pages of Indian books to bind them together. Despite wrapping their books in cloth, for several hundred years Tibetans continued to draw circles on their pages in deference to the Indian tradition.

Initially, books in Tibet were handwritten, using a mixture of stove black for ink on a very strong but light paper made from a Tibetan grass.

Above: The Tibetan library has a highly decorative verandah with brightly painted pillars and capitals.

Below: Statue of Arya Tara.

Facing page: Tibetans circumambulate the Library early morning and evening, thinking good thoughts. The Library is also regarded as a holy place.

The Nechung Monastery in Dharamsala is the seat of the State Oracle.

Both, copying out scriptures and sponsoring their production, were regarded as acts of piety. In due course, books became more elaborate—like the illustrated manuscripts of medieval Europe. They included illustrated title pages bearing the title in Sanskrit and its translation into Tibetan, featuring intricate, coloured paintings, often related to the Buddha. Subsequent pages might also be written in alternating lines of gold and silver on a blue background.

With the introduction of block printing from China, the scriptures could be reproduced as standard editions. But even this method required a huge investment of skilled labour. Every folio was represented by a single wood block with the front page on one side and the back on the other. The words were written in reverse on the wood and then carefully carved out. Printing was done entirely by hand, so block printing did not suddenly lead to mass production. But it did allow for the production of exact copies. Previously, if a monastery had wanted to acquire a particular book or collection of books, it would have borrowed an existing version from another monastery and made a handwritten copy. Inevitably, in the course of writing by hand, some earlier mistakes might have been corrected, but

others would have been introduced, giving rise continually to variant editions.

In the 13th and 14th centuries CE, an indigenous Tibetan literature began to emerge. Teachers and scholars had assimilated Buddhist culture sufficiently and had the confidence to write their own books. Consequently, besides the *Kangyur* and *Tengyur,* the two collections of scriptures translated largely from Indian sources, Tibetan literature expanded with the collected works of particular teachers. The manuscript room of the Tibetan Library contains several editions of the *Kangyur,* a couple of editions of the *Tengyur* and many collections of works brought out of Tibet which were written by illustrious lamas. This is one of the most precious collections of Tibetan books anywhere in the world.

Upstairs, in the centre of the building, a large hall contains the museum which is home to several hundred typically Tibetan Buddhist statues. Most households in Tibet would have had some form of household altar containing a statue of the Buddha or some other religious figure. In these cabinets are statues of the historical Buddha and Bodhisattvas or meditational deities who embody particular qualities: one such example is

Ex-prisoners of the Chinese in Tibet, these Tibetans now find useful employment in exile by working in a bakery.

Pages 56-57: A ritual at Nechung Monastery, led by the medium of the State Oracle.

Prayers and offerings at a Long Life ceremony being performed at the Kalachakra Temple.

that of Manjushri who wields the sword of wisdom which cuts through ignorance. These figures are distinguished by their characteristics, by the hand gestures and the implements that they carry, which represent qualities to which a spiritual practitioner might aspire. The latter may either address prayers to, or meditate on such a figure, visualising the figure in front of himself or visualising himself as one of these forms. These statues are not mere works of art, but religious objects. They are hollow and must be filled with rolls of scriptures and other substances such as incense before they are regarded as properly complete. The faces are painted, often with gold, by artists whose final task is to open—that is to paint in—their eyes. They are consecrated by monks who say prayers over or before them.

The museum also possesses a fine collection of *thangkas*. Some of these are packed with detail, particularly when they depict stories of the life of the Buddha or other spiritual teachers. Others function more as supports for meditational practice, portraying the meditational deity that the meditator visualises in his or her practice. Typically this *thangka* is hung in front of or in view of the meditator's seat. *Thangka* paintings may also be commissioned when there is a need to generate spiritual merit, for example, when a relative or friend has died.

Unique to this museum are two quite different examples of three-dimensional *mandalas*. One is carved of wood and represents the celestial residence of the deity of compassion, Avalokiteshvara. It has all the qualities of an ideal residence. Like the two-dimensional *thangka* painting, it serves to stimulate a meditator's imagination. The second *mandala* belongs to Arya Tara, the female embodiment of the Buddha's virtuous activity. It is created in the unusual medium known as thread cross, in which the planes consist of coloured threads wound on a light frame.

Besides its rich collection of religious objects, the museum also exhibits a collection of tea bowls, some of them porcelain, on elaborate stands with the requisite lid to keep the tea warm. Tea was the staple drink of Tibet. It is said that you could travel the length and breadth of the country carrying only a bag of *tsampa,* roasted barley flour, and your tea bowl. That would be sufficient, because you would be offered tea wherever you were.

The Tibetan Library is the focus of several other activities including classes by qualified lamas on Buddhist philosophy, from Tibetan texts translated into English. These classes have continued since the very foundation of the Library in 1971 and have been attended by hundreds of people from all over the world.

An ongoing project involves making audio recordings of the stories and recollections of a wide cross-section of the Tibetan society who can remember life in old Tibet. A team of old gentlemen well qualified to write Tibetan are steadily transcribing many of these reminiscences so that they may eventually be published. Elsewhere in the complex, work goes on: translating Tibetan books into English, teaching Tibetan language and preparing material for publication.

Nechung Monastery

Another ritual being performed at the Nechung Monastery. This ceremony is also led by the State Oracle.

Below the Library of Tibetan Works and Archives, but still within the compound of the Tibetan government-in-exile, stands Nechung, the small monastery of the state oracle. There has been a close connection between this oracle and its presiding, protective spirit going back to the Great Fifth Dalai Lama, the first person to have governed a unified Tibet since the disintegration of the original Tibetan empire in the 8th-9th centuries. The state oracle's responsibility is to advise the Tibetan government and ensure its welfare. The temple at Nechung has been constructed with great care in the traditional manner but with modern materials. Visitors are very likely to find one of the cycle of rituals performed by the monks throughout the year going on here, to the strident accompaniment of horns, drums and cymbals.

Over the last thirty years Dharamsala has attracted people from the world over with an interest in Tibetan Buddhism and Tibetan culture. Many have attended classes at the Library of Tibetan Works and Archives and studied traditional Buddhist culture as it was preserved in Tibet. Some who have wished to put this experience into practice in actual meditation have participated in courses at the Tushita Meditation Centre which is perched above McLeod Ganj on the road to Triond. Presently there are facilities for individual meditators to go into retreat, and opportunities for people to attend group retreats with access to advice from experienced meditators.

The Tibetan Medical Centre (Men-tsee-khang)

Precious Tibetan medicine for nerve disorders. Tibetan medicine is especially effective for disorders of the digestive and nervous systems and liver ailments.

Facing page: Counting of Tibetan medicine. Tibetan medicine believes in restoring balance of health.

Pages 62-63: The main street of McLeod Ganj, heart of the Tibetan community-in-exile. Some devoted Tibetans spin the prayer wheels that flank the Namgyal Stupa in the heart of the village. Others make their way home after teachings at the Tsuglagkhang.

The Tibetan Medical and Astrological Centre was established in exile to preserve the traditions that had been the responsibility of the Medical College on Chagpori hill in Lhasa since it was founded by *Desi* Sangye Gyatso, the regent of the Fifth Dalai Lama in the seventeenth century. The Men-tsee-khang continues to train doctors, pharmacists and astrologers, besides producing traditional Tibetan medicine, calendars, horoscopes, and so forth. The public can attend the clinic: a doctor examines the pulse in the patient's wrist and perhaps a sample of the first urine of the day. From this he or she can diagnose the patient's condition and prescribe various medicines, dietary advice such as avoiding oily food, and behavioural recommendations such as keeping the stomach warm or drinking hot rather than cold water.

The Tibetan medical system is very effective in treating digestive and nervous disorders and remarkably effective in dealing with hepatitis and other liver ailments. The Tibetan medical system can often help where Western medicine has little to offer. Whereas a Western doctor may tell you to come back in a week if you feel no better, a Tibetan physician can immediately pinpoint what is wrong and give you something to restore the balance of your health.

The astrological department can be approached to cast a horoscope, although this may require more faith than Tibetan medicine does. This department is also responsible for drawing up the popular Tibetan calendar annually. Following a lunar system as it does, it requires recalculation every year. Since months do not necessarily consist of a regular number of days, the astrological department has to calculate when some dates will be repeated and others will be missing. For example, for reasons of auspiciousness, the nineteenth may occur twice in one month, but the twelfth may be missing from another.

The Men-tsee-khang also incorporates the largest Tibetan pharmacy outside Tibet; it has been partly automated with equipment supplied from Germany. At certain times of the year, the staff goes up into the hills around Dharamsala, as well as around Lahaul and Manali, to gather leaves, flowers and other parts of plants to be made into medicines. In the recently opened museum, the medical *tantras,* which are the fundamental texts of this medical system, are vividly displayed as *thangkas.* Another interesting painting shows the process of conception, gestation and birth. Two cabinets contain all the texts that someone studying as a doctor or as an astrologer must master. There are also fascinating displays of the various mineral and herbal substances that go into the making of the medicines.

Traditional Tibetan Physicians

McLeod Ganj is host to a number of Tibetan doctors. Dr Yeshe Dhonden, for example, is definitely one of the more-famous personalities of McLeod Ganj. He trained at Lhasa's principal medical college on Chakpori Hill with one of the great physicians of the early part of the century. In exile he served as personal physician to the Dalai Lama and continues to practice in Dharamsala where he is consulted by people interested in Tibetan medicine. He can look you in the eye, take your pulse, examine a specimen of your urine and give you an account of the present state of your health and of past ailments reaching back into your childhood. Not only can he recognise what is wrong with you, but he also prescribes gentle remedies to set you right.

McLeod Ganj - The Namgyal Stupa

As you walk through the village of McLeod Ganj, the most prominent landmark is the Namgyal stupa or *chorten*, a typical Buddhist reliquary monument standing in the middle of the main street. Monuments like this are to be found wherever Buddhism has spread, providing a focus for the physical aspect of spiritual practice. People bow down before the stupa and circumambulate it. In the early days, the stupa was surrounded by an open area, where people would gather to pray for the welfare of Tibet and the people left behind. As time went on, ceremonial elaboration began to include the erection of prayer wheels: brass drums which spin on a well-oiled axis

Thangka *painting of Kalachakra and lineage hanging in the temple at Norbulingka Institute.*

containing large rolls of printed mantras and prayers, such as the name mantra of Guru Padmasambhava and the six-syllable mantra of Avalokiteshvara—the Bodhisattva of compassion, who is virtually the patron deity of Tibet. As people walk around the stupa, they spin the prayer wheels, turn a rosary in their hands, and recite prayers and mantras to themselves. This simple procedure involves the activities of body, speech and mind in spiritual practice.

A thangka being painted at the Norbulingka studio.

Norbulingka Institute

During the nineties, there has been a substantial increase in the number of Tibetans on the outskirts of Dharamsala. Down on the floor of the valley is the Norbulingka Institute, which is dedicated to the preservation of Tibetan art and culture. It is a large, beautiful place, whose buildings reflect the Tibetan style with broad walls richly decorated by the institute's own artists and which taper towards the top. The main complex has a unique ground plan laid out according to the shape of the deity of compassion, Avalokiteshvara, with eleven heads and a thousand arms.

Passing through the Institute's gateway, visitors are immediately impressed by the peaceful atmosphere of the lush green gardens. In this the

Mural paintings of Indian Buddhist geshis at the Norbulingka Institute.

Norbulingka Institute emulates the park of the same name near Lhasa that was the location of the Dalai Lama's summer palaces. The original Norbulingka was established by the seventh Dalai Lama in the 18th century to consolidate the artistic traditions of Tibet out of concern to preserve the quality of Tibetan art. The Norbulingka Institute aims to provide a supportive environment which emulates the guild system of artists and apprentices that existed in Tibet. Teams of artists are able to take on much grander commissions than an individual artist could; this gives the artists much greater scope and experience to develop their skills.

There are several workshops within the complex. One creates tents similar to those used in Lhasa for extensive picnics. In another, items from elaborate dolls houses to simple trays are decorated by hand. Another workshop preserves the traditional craft of making appliqué *thangkas*. This is painstaking work in which the piping is still made from horsehair and all the pieces are sewn together rather than glued. The huge *thangkas* made in this way are displayed during specific festivals. Several monasteries-in-exile have commissioned large *thangkas* here. The Institute also maintains a *thangka* painting studio (where you can observe artists of all levels of skill—from those who are just beginning to draw, to fully qualified master artists) besides wood carving and metal craft workshops.

The Institute's Academy of Tibetan Culture offers young people, who have completed their school education, the opportunity to train in higher

A colossal gilded copper statue of the Buddha that is the focus of the Seat of Happerim Temple at the Norbulingka Institute.

Facing page: Several monasteries have commissioned large thangkas *at the Norbulingka Institute.*

Many of the nuns at Dolma Ling had demonstrated against Chinese rule in Tibet and were consequently harshly treated. They arrived in India traumatised. At Dolma Ling they have found a degree of security once more.

Tibetan studies, in literary skills, such as poetics, history and philosophy. The aim is to train young people in the finer points of their own culture and enable them to express it in a global context.

A Literary and Cultural Research Centre employs a team of young researchers and writers, most of who were trained in Tibet, but who were unable to find any fruitful expression of their knowledge there because the Tibetan language is virtually suppressed in Tibet. This team of young writers puts together a monthly cultural newspaper in Tibetan, an annual journal of scholarly writing in Tibetan and a youth magazine. They are working to produce a Tibetan encyclopaedia in three volumes.

The Losel Dolls Museum houses a unique collection of nearly 150 exhibition dolls that depict the costumes of the different regions and various aspects of Tibetan society. They

Togdem yogis from Tash'long, below Dharamsala in the Kangra Valley.

showcase how people actually used to dress in the local regions of Tibet before the Chinese takeover of the country. Great efforts have been made to ensure accuracy and that the materials are authentic. The dolls are made by a team of monks from the Drepung Loseling Monastery, which has been re-established in Karnataka, south India. The monks employ skills they already have: modelling, sewing and painting. Older Tibetans are often tearful at seeing things they had almost forgotten and children are awestruck at seeing things they have only heard about from their parents and grandparents.

The focus of the main Norbulingka complex is the Seat of Happiness Temple. The four traditional temple guardians, the guardians of the four directions, stand watch over the entrance. Once you step over the threshold of the brightly painted main doorway, you are immediately struck by the colossal statue of the traditional Buddha, Shakyamuni, which sits on a raised dais against the rear wall. This 14-feet, gilded copper statue was constructed within the temple itself by a team of statue makers, led by master Pemba Dorjee. He was also responsible for the statues in the Thekchen Chöling temple and is regarded as the only living master of this statue-making tradition in exile.

Work on this grand image took more than a year. The statue was fashioned from copper sheets, each piece being cut and worked on individually until it was ready to be gilded in a process using gold and mercury. The burnished parts were then assembled into the complete statue. During the assembly the statue was filled with precious and medicinal substances and collections of religious texts. Even the base was filled with various offerings, one level containing pieces of jewellery contributed by members of the Norbulingka community.

There are more than a thousand images in the murals lining the walls of the temple. Behind the Buddha statue a series of paintings depicts the twelve principal deeds of the Buddha's life from conception in his mother's

Left and facing page: Making stamped clay images of the deities of Long Life.

Pages 72-73: Tibetans nuns studying scriptural texts at Dolma Ling Nunnery.

womb, through his attaining enlightenment, to his passing away. Flanking them are paintings of the sixteen *arhats* who were the Buddha's principal disciples. Unique to this temple are a set of paintings of the fourteen Dalai Lamas around the upper balcony. The Great Fifth is on the eastern wall facing the Thirteenth and the Fourteenth Dalai Lamas, represented in actual likeness. Following the conventional pattern, the temple is crowned by an apartment for honoured guests, the most important of whom is His Holiness the Dalai Lama.

Dolma Ling Nunnery

Adjacent to the Norbulingka Institute is the Dolma Ling Nunnery which was established in the early 1990s to accommodate the great influx of nuns escaping from Tibet. Many of them had fled following their participation in demonstrations against the Chinese occupation of their homeland and their expulsion from their nunneries. Although many monasteries were re-established in exile, very few nuns arrived before 1991 so there were far fewer places where nuns could receive an education. At

Performers of the Tibetan
Institute of Performing Arts
off duty.

Dolma Ling, nuns are being trained in the Tibetan language and the scriptures and are engaged particularly in the philosophical practice of debate. Until this decade, there was no opportunity for nuns to engage in this traditional form of Buddhist education. While visiting Dolma Ling in the morning, one is likely to find the nuns in their classrooms, but in the afternoon, the courtyards come alive with clusters of nuns engaged in lively formal discussion of the topics they have been studying.

The Tibetan Institute of Performing Arts

The origins of the Tibetan Institute of Performing Arts (TIPA) go back to the early sixties, when the Tibetan Dance and Drama Society was founded in Kalimpong. The establishment of this institution is an indication that albeit very religious, preserving religion was not the only thing that concerned Tibetans. The performing arts, like so much else in Tibetan life, have strong religious associations, yet they reveal the lighter side of the culture. Tibetans are, in fact, quite happy to take things easy and enjoy themselves.

Performers of the Tibetan Institute of Performing Arts with their masks.

Shortly after the Dalai Lama settled in Dharamsala, TIPA was transferred here and has grown from strength to strength. It preserves the Lhamo opera, which began at the time of the great adept Tangthong Gyalpo, who travelled around 14th-15th-century Tibet improving communications by building bridges. His opera troupe came about when he gathered a group of girls to sing and dance for people in an attempt to raise funds for building a bridge. He trained them to perform so sweetly that people said that watching them was like being in the presence of goddesses or Lhamo. This is why the opera tradition is referred to today as Lhamo. Many of the performances tell stories based on Buddhist myths. Besides being entertaining there is always a moral to edify the audience.

TIPA maintains a wide range of associated traditions including singing and dancing, production and maintenance of the wonderful rich costumes and musical instruments. The Institute also trains people in the traditions of folk song and basic musicianship. Graduates go out into the Tibetan settlements in India and Nepal as teachers. Thus, there is a constant effort to keep these traditions alive. The Institute also provides specialist services, such as the formal welcoming ceremony when His Holiness the Dalai Lama is visiting or attending a particular function. During the Losar or Tibetan New Year celebrations, they are responsible for the court music at certain points in the proceedings and perform a special dance in the temple.

Tibetan Children's Village band leads proceedings on the Tibetan Uprising Day on 10th March.

Similarly, on occasions such as the Tibetan Uprising Day, 10th March, and His Holiness's birthday, 6th July, they lead the singing of the National Anthem. In Tibet a major opera festival called the Shotun or Yogurt Festival took place annually at the Norbulingka under the auspices of Drepung Monastery. TIPA today holds a Shotun festival early in the Tibetan new year, generally soon after the spring teachings that accompany the Great Prayer Festival.

The Tibetan Institute of Performing Arts provides training for musicians.

Facing page: A musician of the Tibetan Institute of Performing Arts, dressed in traditional costume, plays the phi-warg.

The Tibetan Children's Village

The first Tibetan Children's Village (TCV) was established very early on in 1960-61 at the present site above Tanglewood led by the first Principal, His Holiness's elder sister, Tsering Dolma. She created the pattern for subsequent TCVs. One of their most important functions was as an orphanage. Many of the children who, born in Tibet, had escaped into exile, were left bereft because their parents succumbed to the trauma of their escape, the rigours of the climate, and various diseases such as tuberculosis. Consequently, there were many orphans. TCV was set up as a group of family homes, each with house parents, who looked after the two-dozen or

Calisthenic performance during the anniversary celebrations of the Tibetan Children's Village (TCV).

so children living in their house. This provided them the opportunity of bringing up the children with Tibetan values and giving them some semblance of family life.

Many capable adults offered their services as teachers and, between them, they managed to set up a syllabus based on the Indian model, but tailored to suit Tibetan children with an emphasis on Tibetan studies. These were the circumstances under which the first generation of Tibetan children-in-exile, many of whom now hold responsible positions in the exile community, were educated.

Later, there were far fewer orphans. In the late seventies and early eighties, TCV became more like a boarding school for Tibetan refugee children. Then, in the mid-eighties, following a relaxation of restrictions in Tibet, there was a new influx of children from Tibet, seeking the education they were denied in their homeland.

For nearly 20 years there was very little communication between the community in Dharamsala and their families in Tibet. With the end of the cultural revolution, the easing of restrictions in Tibet and the opportunity for the government-in-exile to send in fact-finding missions, links were restored once more. Consequently, in the eighties, many Tibetan families brought their children out of Tibet to Dharamsala to ensure that they received a Tibetan education. This is still happening today.

Today, TCV provides opportunities for students to receive either an academic education or a vocational training according to their

A young artist from the Tibetan Institute of Performing Arts, waits to perform in the temple during Losar (New Year) celebrations.

Facing page, top: A flutist from the Tibetan Institute of Performing Arts plays at the Himalayan Festival.

Facing page, bottom: At the opera.

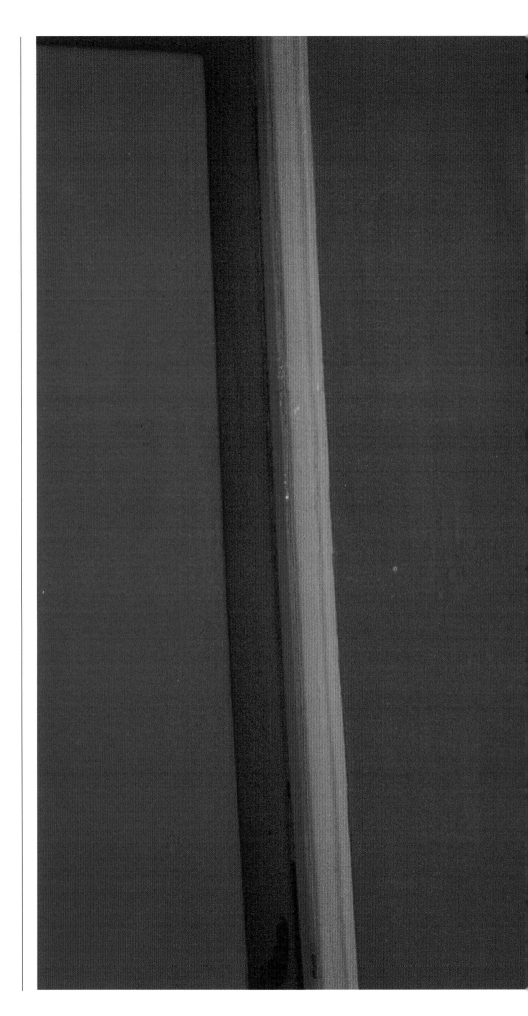

A young Tibetan Buddhist monk.

aptitude, but most of all, it inculcates in them a sense of their Tibetan identity. This is what makes it one of the major Tibetan institutions in Dharamsala.

Carpet Weaving

✝

One of the mainstays of the Tibetan economy is the production of carpets. There are several private and cooperative carpet-weaving enterprises in Dharamsala, as there are in many of the other settlements scattered through India and Nepal. They are quite different from the carpet factories that are the butt of criticism elsewhere, because the Tibetan carpet is thick and loosely knotted and is quite easily woven by adults sitting together at their looms in an enjoyable, friendly atmosphere.

Traditional carpets mostly consist of the 6-feet by 3-feet bed carpets, because in Tibet it is far too cold to sit on the bare ground. The point is not to carpet the floor, but to have a rug on the bed on which one can sit during the day and sleep at night. Here, in India, weavers have been able to expand their repertoire and produce carpets of a much greater variety. Another feature of Tibetan carpets is the clipping out of the pattern, which has an almost sculptural effect of enhancing the design. While women often do the weaving, men do the final clipping of the carpet. Nothing is wasted, because the clippings of wool are collected to make an excellent warm filling for cushions and mattresses.

Above and pages 88-89: Clipping out the pattern of a completed carpet in a carpet factory.

Facing page: Musical performance at the anniversary celebrations of the TCV.

Below: Dragon head water spout. Dragons are regarded as the protectors of the celestial realms. Dragon dribble is called norbu *(wish-fulfilling gem). Dragon bones are coveted by Tibetan doctors for their healing powers.*

Around Dharamsala

✝

There are several attractive places to walk to from McLeod Ganj and Dharamsala. One of the most charming is the spring and the temple of Bhagsunath. Legend has it that a king came here from Rajasthan in search of water for his drought-stricken people. He found water at this point and miraculously gathered it all into his bowl with the intention of taking it back to his suffering people. But he caught the attention of the powerful resident *naga*, the serpentine being who represented the spirit of the water source. Sorely displeased by the king's effrontery, it attacked and defeated him. The king pleaded that he had intended no harm and requested that at least his name should not be forgotten. Thus it was that the *naga* allowed King Bhagsu's name to be attached to his own, creating the name Bhagsunag or Bhagsunath.

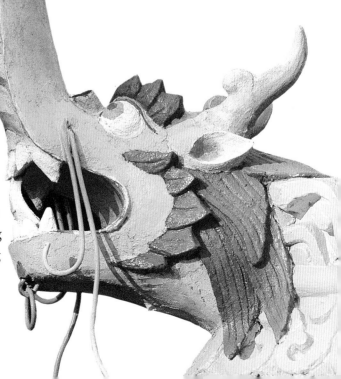

Working at the loom in a carpet factory at Dharamsala. There are several carpet-weaving factories in Dharamsala.

Many legends relate the power of this *naga*. Local people typically offer the first milk of their cow at the temple. It is said that in the course of a tussle, a king's bowl fell and some milk was spilt. A fresh-water spring came forth, which can now be seen flowing into the tank. Devout Hindus regard it as having sacred qualities and can be seen taking a holy dip in the water. Behind Bhagsunath a high waterfall pours into the Churan Khud, the thieving river which conceals its flow beneath its sandy bed except during the monsoon when it roars forth in a raging torrent. High above are the slate quarries which provide the high-quality tiles for local roofs.

A three-to-four-hour brisk walk out of McLeod Ganj brings you to Triond, a col at nearly 10,000 feet above sea level. From the verandah of the Forest Rest House can be seen picturesque views of the Kangra Valley down to the Pong Dam lake. There is also a precipitous path to the Indrahar pass, by which foolhardy trekkers and Gaddi shepherds cross the Dhauladhar mountains to reach Brahmour and Chamba beyond.

The Mall Road leading out of McLeod Ganj towards TCV leads to the Dal Lake which is regarded locally as sacred. Its edge is dotted with small temples and its waters are populated by large somnolent carp. The road finally ends on the ridge of Talnu from where the most glorious views of the sunset can be seen. Descending from this point through wooded villages, a shepherd's track leads to the alpine lake of Kareri Dal and the Minkiani pass beyond it.

Beyond Kotwali bazaar, Dharamsala's main market, lie the pine-wooded slopes of the Chilgari estate, the location of the senior civil officers' residences. This gives way to one of the original British tea gardens which continues to be cultivated and produces the famous local Kangra tea. At the far edge of the garden stands the celebrated Kunal Patri temple, the focus of a local Spring fair.

The Kangra Art Museum on the edge of Kotwali Bazaar has a substantial permanent exhibition of Kangra miniature paintings. The last independent king of Kangra, Sansar Chand, was a leading patron of these paintings. These paintings are peculiar to the Himachal region and, following the style of Persian miniatures, represent one of the areas in which Hindu and Muslim traditions combined. In addition to Hindu religious themes, these paintings may depict the mood of a musical *raga*. The museum displays statues and other archaeological findings unearthed in the Kangra valley and also functions as a gallery for local contemporary artists.

The lower reaches of Dharamsala are home to the offices of the civil administration, the Forestry Department, the Police Station, the Main Post Office, the Zonal Hospital, the Medical College, the College and the Post Graduate College. A sombre war memorial commemorates those who died in the wars with China and Pakistan.

As part of the Tibetan struggle for freedom, there is a move to boycott Chinese goods.

Pages 94-95: Marching and chanting for Tibetan freedom.

The Future

Dharamsala has already gone through several incarnations. With its stunning scenery and comfortable climate, it will continue to attract people in search of respite from the heat and dust, the pollution, and the hustle and bustle of the cities of the plains. As for the Tibetans, His Holiness the Dalai Lama has, for forty years, spoken optimistically of returning to Tibet during his lifetime. He says: 'The return of freedom to our homeland is what so many Tibetans, men and women alike, have struggled for years in many different ways to achieve. I pray that as a culmination of all these efforts, our dream may soon be fulfilled.'

ISBN : 0-89346-920-3

© **Roli Books Pvt. Ltd. 2000**
Lustre Press Pvt. Ltd.

First American Edition 2000
00 01 02 03 04 05 10 9 8 7 6 5 4 3 2 1

HEIAN INTERNATIONAL, INC.
1815 West 205th Street, Suite #301
Torrance, CA 90501

Web Site: www.heian.com
E-mail: heianemail@heian.com

Foreword:
His Holiness the Dalai Lama

Text:
Jeremy Russell

Photo Credits:
Angus McDonald: 12-13, 18-19 (2 pix), 20, 23, 24, 25 (top), 43, 48, 49, 65, 80-81, 82 (top), 86, 87 (top), 88-89, 90-91
Diane Barker: 1, 2, 25 (bottom), 58
James Barllam Brown: 30-31 (3 pix), 66, 70, 71, 94-95
Rajiv Mehrotra: 32-33
Lustre Collection: 22, 34-35, 36-37, 38, 39, 40-41, 46-47, 52, 53, 54-55, 56-57, 59, 64, 67, 87 (bottom)
Thomas L. Kelly: 4-5, 10-11, 16-17, 21, 26 (top & bottom), 27 (top & bottom), 28-29, 41, 42, 44, 45, 50, 51, 55, 60, 61, 68, 69, 72-73, 74, 75, 76-77, 79, 82 (bottom), 83, 84-85, 92, 93
Tibet Image Bank:
Diana Barker: 6, 9, 14-15, 78, Edwin Maynard: 62-63

Printed and bound in Singapore

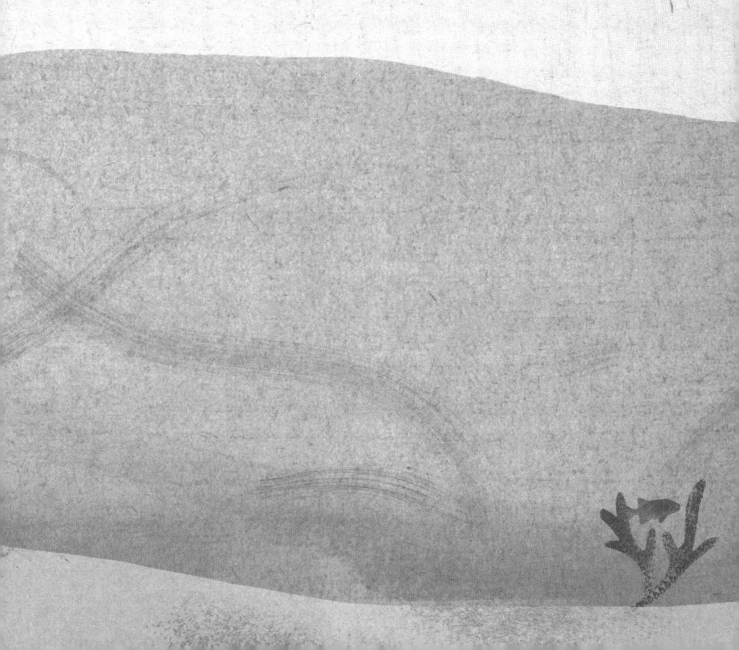

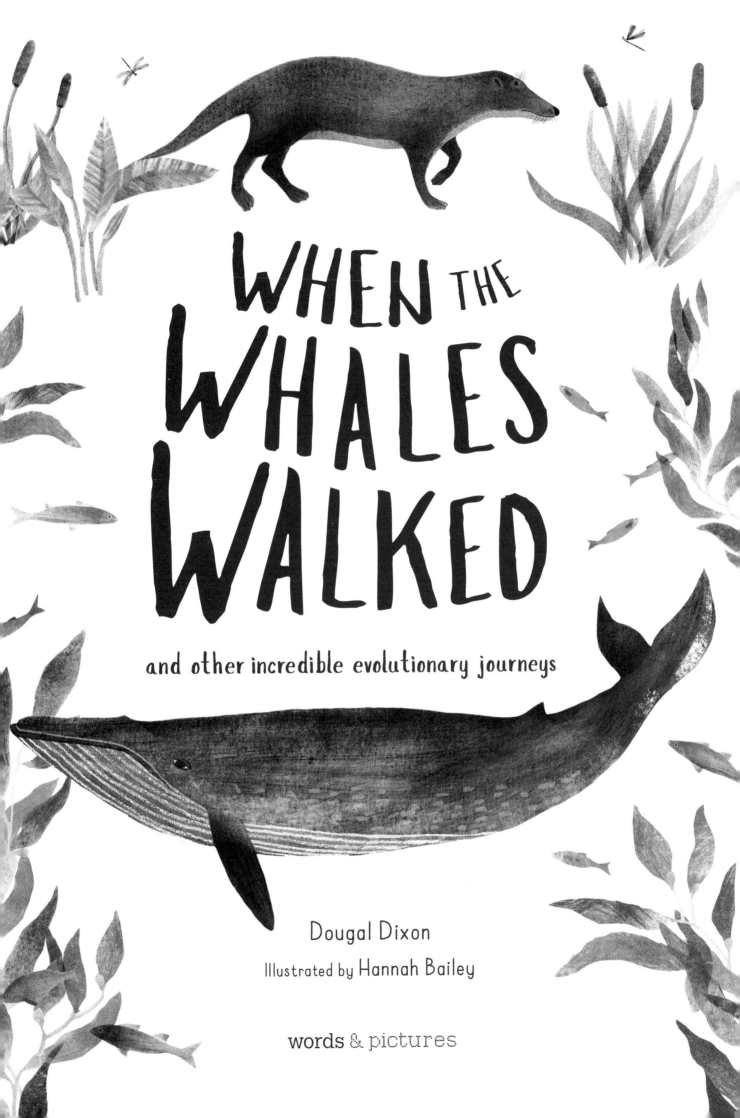

WHEN THE WHALES WALKED

and other incredible evolutionary journeys

Dougal Dixon

Illustrated by Hannah Bailey

words & pictures

Quarto Knows

Quarto is the authority on a wide range of topics.

Quarto educates, entertains and enriches the lives of our readers—enthusiasts and lovers of hands-on living.

www.quartoknows.com

First published in 2018 by words & pictures,
an imprint of The Quarto Group.
6 Orchard Road, Suite 100
Lake Forest, CA 92630
T: +1 949 380 7510
F: +1 949 380 7575
www.QuartoKnows.com

Designer: Anna Lubeka
Editorial Director: Laura Knowles
Art Director: Susi Martin
Creative Director: Malena Stojic
Publisher: Maxime Boucknooghe

A CIP record for this book is available from the Library of Congress.

ISBN 978-1-912413-97-3

Manufactured in Guangdong, China CC112020

9 8 7 6 5 4 3

FSC
MIX
Paper from
responsible sources
FSC® C008047

CONTENTS

WHAT IS EVOLUTION?

Imagine a volcano growing on the ocean floor and erupting through the water's surface. The lava cools, forming a new island. A flock of birds have been blown off course in their migration, and they stop to rest on the new island. The only food available is the shrimp that wash up on the shore. Only a few of the birds have a taste for these shrimp. The rest of the flock either dies or flies away to look for food elsewhere.

The birds that are left lay eggs. Some of the chicks will have a taste for the shrimp and so they can feed. Others are like the rest of the original flock—they cannot eat them, so they die. Only those that can eat the shrimp grow up and have chicks of their own.

After many years, only the shrimp-eating birds have survived. The descendants of the rest of the original flock come back to the island, having been blown off course again. They find that their distant relatives who stayed have become so different that they have become a different species. This is evolution.

Changing and adapting

Evolution can happen anywhere and at any time, not just on a new island. Any change in habitat or climate can spark evolution. An animal does not decide to evolve. It is a process that happens gradually, through small changes over many generations.

Mutations

When animals have babies, most of their offspring are very similar to their parents and can live in the same environment. Occasionally there will be a random change in the genes that control a baby animal's traits. This kind of change is called a mutation. Most mutations make the animal less likely to survive. If the animal dies, or does not have babies of its own, the mutation cannot be passed on.

However, once in a while, the mutation will actually give the animal an advantage. The animal will survive and will likely have lots of healthy offspring of its own, passing on its useful mutation. We call this process natural selection, and it is how evolution works. Mutations produce changes, and natural selection leads to more animals with the successful mutations.

The journey begins...

This book will take you on a tour of the history of life on Earth, following all of its twists and turns. The thirteen case studies each describe the evolution of a different group of animals, from the earliest fish to modern humans. As you uncover the history of each group, see if you can spot the patterns in the ways that different animals have evolved.

A TIMELINE OF LIFE ON EARTH

There has been life on Earth ever since the planet was cool enough and stable enough to support it—about three and a half billion years. The timescales are so vast that they are hard to comprehend. To make it easier, scientists divide Earth's history into manageable chunks, or periods. These periods are based on the types of living things that existed during that time.

Geologic time scale, 600 million years ago to the present

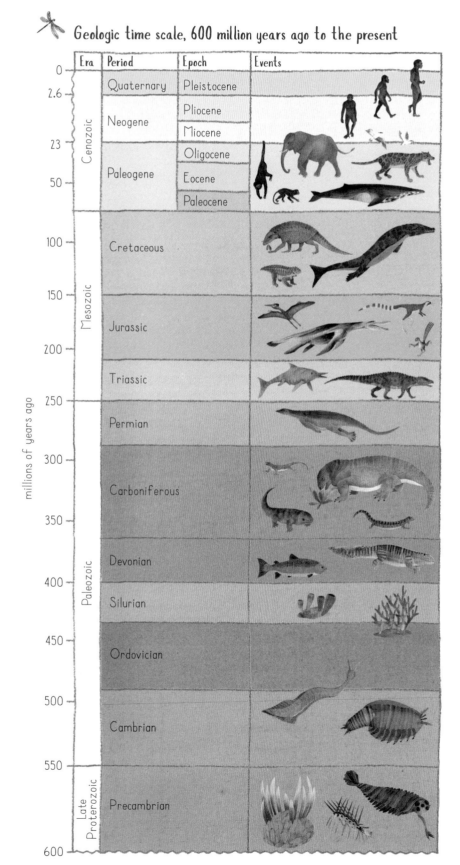

Era	Period	Epoch	Events
Cenozoic	Quaternary	Pleistocene	
	Neogene	Pliocene	
		Miocene	
	Paleogene	Oligocene	
		Eocene	
		Paleocene	
Mesozoic	Cretaceous		
	Jurassic		
	Triassic		
Paleozoic	Permian		
	Carboniferous		
	Devonian		
	Silurian		
	Ordovician		
	Cambrian		
Late Proterozoic	Precambrian		

millions of years ago

(scale marks: 0, 2.6, 23, 50, 100, 150, 200, 250, 300, 350, 400, 450, 500, 550, 600)

As long as there has been life, there has been evolution. For most of Earth's history, the only life forms that existed were simple organisms made up of a single cell. More complex living things appeared about 600 million years ago (MYA).

The chart on the left shows the geological time scale of life on Earth from this point onward. The time scale is always laid out like this, with the oldest living things at the bottom and the youngest at the top. This reflects the sequence in which the Earth's rocks were laid down.

WHERE DO FOSSILS COME FROM?

Fossils are the remains of living things that have been preserved in rock. Most fossils are found in sea sediments. In fact, until about 400 million years ago all life was in the water. After this, fossils of land plants and animals begin to appear, but these fossils are very rare compared with those of sea-dwellers.

EARTH TODAY

North America
Europe
Asia
Africa
South America
Australia
Antarctica

CRETACEOUS PERIOD
66 MILLION YEARS AGO

North America
Asia
Europe
South America
Africa
India
Australia
Antarctica

JURASSIC PERIOD
145 MILLION YEARS AGO

Laurasia
Gondwana

PERMIAN PERIOD
250 MILLION YEARS AGO

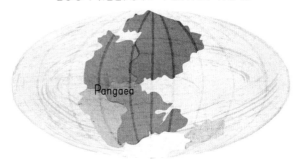

Pangaea

SILURIAN PERIOD
419 MILLION YEARS AGO

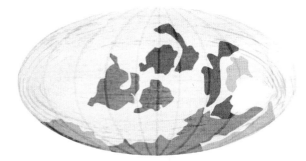

Changing Earth

It is not only life that has been changing—the surface of the planet has been changing too. Millions of years ago, there were several large continents scattered across the globe. They were moving all the time, "floating" on the softer rock deep inside Earth. About 335 million years ago, all the continents came together and fused into a single "supercontinent" which we call Pangaea.

Pangaea existed for about 60 million years, and then, in the middle of the Jurassic period, it began to split. The landmasses slowly drifted apart, giving us the continents that we know today. Have you ever wondered why the eastern coast of South America seems to be a perfect fit with the western coast of Africa? They were joined together, long ago. The continents are still moving, but very slowly—about 1 inch (2.5 cm) per year.

All change

Today, each corner of the world is home to very different animals. Millions of years ago, different kinds of animals lived on different continents, but they mixed with other species as continents came together. They then became separated when the continents split up again. Continents' climates changed as they moved between the hot tropics and cold polar regions. These changing conditions, combined with natural selection, produced the huge variety of life we see today.

WORKING OUT THE EVOLUTIONARY TREE

The idea of evolution—one group of animals changing into another—has been around for a long time. However, it was British scientist Charles Darwin (1809-82) who really brought it to people's attention with his book *On The Origin of Species*, published in 1859.

Darwin is usually credited as being the first person to realise that the process of evolution requires a combination of mutation and natural selection. But great minds think alike—another scientist, Alfred Russell Wallace, was working in a different part of the world, and he came up with the same idea at the same time.

The tree of life

Darwin didn't picture evolution working as a single line, with one animal changing into another and then into another. Instead, he saw it as more like a tree or a bush. There were various lines branching off in different directions. Most of them died out, but some carried on and survived. Each surviving branch was capable of splitting into more branches.

Darwin's idea of a "tree of life" soon became the standard way of illustrating evolutionary history, and it lasted for about a hundred years. The various branches on the tree were based on fossil evidence and could be fitted neatly into the geological timescale. Fossil hunters searched for new discoveries that would serve as the "missing link" to show how one animal evolved into another. The diagram shown here is a very simple tree of life that focuses on the animals discussed in this book. A full tree of life would have many more branches, and would also include all plants and microorganisms.

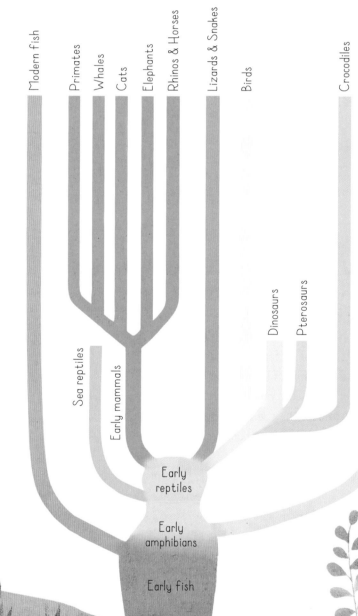

Cladograms

Today's scientists often focus on a single family or group of animals, using a diagram called a cladogram. To draw a cladogram, they take the features of different animals and compare them with one another. By counting the similarities, they can figure out which animals are more closely related than others.

Modern cladograms can be built by analyzing an animal's DNA—the genetic makeup of their cells. Using DNA, scientists can often tell how far back in time one family of animals diverged from another.

What does "MYA" mean?

You'll see the letters MYA after many of the dates in this book. MYA stands for "millions of years ago." The dates given are always approximate. They're worked out by dating fossils, but the fewer the fossils found, the less there is to go on.

Throughout Earth's history, many strange and beautiful animal species have roamed the planet. Some of them were evolutionary dead ends, but others evolved further, becoming the species that we know today. Now that you know how evolution works, it's time to see it in action!

Are you ready? Then let's go back in time!

Sea reptiles

Lizards & Snakes

Crocodiles

Pterosaurs

Birds

Dinosaurs

Elephants

Rhinos & Horses

Cats

Whales

Primates

AMNIOTES

ARCHOSAURS

MAMMALS

NATURE'S BIG EXPERIMENT

Something strange happened about 540 million years ago. Hard shells suddenly evolved. This might not sound all that impressive, but it had a big impact. Before this, animal life consisted of soft squishy things, built like little pillows, with flexible outer coverings and squashy organs inside. Hardly anything was fossilized. Now, with hard shells, things could be preserved as fossils, and from this point onward we have a clear idea of how life evolved.

Trial and error

The hard shell or skeleton was so successful that it allowed all sorts of new things to evolve. Nature seemed to be trying out all sorts of shapes and lifestyles to see what worked. Most of these new creatures were not successful, but some went on to evolve into the many animals that we see around us today.

Strange fossils

The evolution of hard shells marks the beginning of what we call the Cambrian period. On the side of a mountain in British Columbia, Canada, there is a sequence of Cambrian rocks called the Burgess Shales. These contain the fossils of many strange creatures that evolved in the oceans at this time. Here are just a few!

HALLUCIGENIA

Pronounced: Hal-oo-si-jen-eye-a
Size: 1 inch (3 cm) long

Hallucigenia had tentacles along one side, stilt-like struts along the other, and a trunk at one end. Scientists are still trying to figure out how *Hallucigenia* lived—or even which way up it stood. It only lived in Cambrian times.

OPABINIA

Pronounced: Oh-pa-bin-eea
Size: 3 inches (7 cm) long

This hard-shelled creature had a segmented body, a pair of jaws at the end of a long trunk, possibly gills on the tail, and five eyes. Count them! *Opabinia* did not survive either.

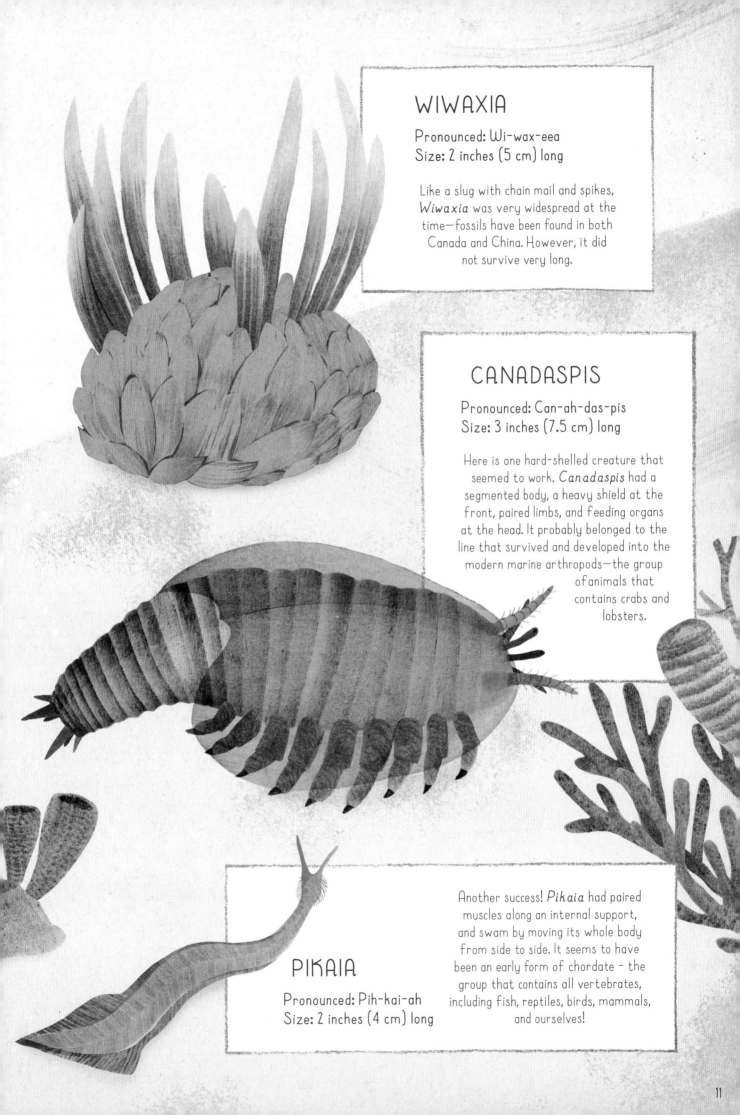

WIWAXIA

Pronounced: Wi-wax-eea
Size: 2 inches (5 cm) long

Like a slug with chain mail and spikes,
Wiwaxia was very widespread at the
time—fossils have been found in both
Canada and China. However, it did
not survive very long.

CANADASPIS

Pronounced: Can-ah-das-pis
Size: 3 inches (7.5 cm) long

Here is one hard-shelled creature that
seemed to work. *Canadaspis* had a
segmented body, a heavy shield at the
front, paired limbs, and feeding organs
at the head. It probably belonged to the
line that survived and developed into the
modern marine arthropods—the group
of animals that
contains crabs and
lobsters.

PIKAIA

Pronounced: Pih-kai-ah
Size: 2 inches (4 cm) long

Another success! *Pikaia* had paired
muscles along an internal support,
and swam by moving its whole body
from side to side. It seems to have
been an early form of chordate - the
group that contains all vertebrates,
including fish, reptiles, birds, mammals,
and ourselves!

WHEN FINS BECAME FEET

For most of Earth's history, all life existed and evolved in the water.
Only about 400 million years ago did things begin to live in the open air.
For all backboned animals, this involved the evolution of lungs. But it
also involved changes to the whole shape of the animal.

WATER VERSUS LAND

Let's look at the differences between
the body shape of a fish, which is
well-adapted to living in water, and a
simple land-living tetrapod: a lizard.

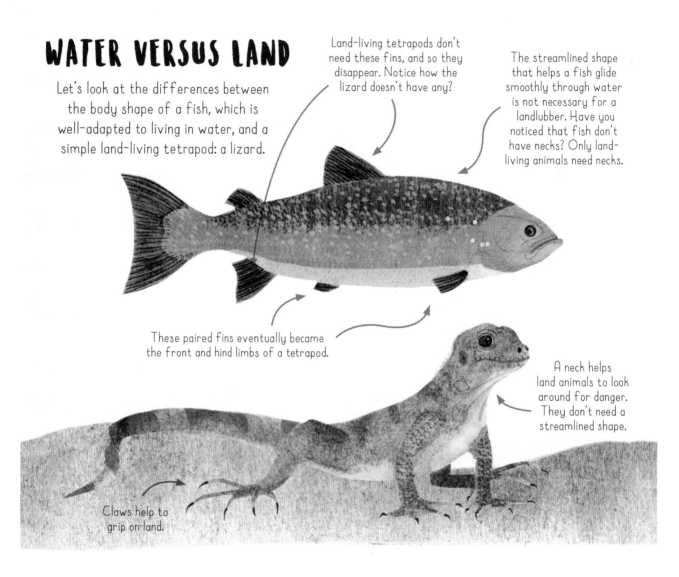

Land-living tetrapods don't
need these fins, and so they
disappear. Notice how the
lizard doesn't have any?

The streamlined shape
that helps a fish glide
smoothly through water
is not necessary for a
landlubber. Have you
noticed that fish don't
have necks? Only land-
living animals need necks.

These paired fins eventually became
the front and hind limbs of a tetrapod.

A neck helps
land animals to look
around for danger.
They don't need a
streamlined shape.

Claws help to
grip on land.

What's a tetrapod?

The name given to land-living
vertebrates is "tetrapod." This literally
means "four feet." It applies even to
things that have only two feet, like
birds, or no feet at all, like snakes!
This is because birds and snakes evolved
from four-footed ancestors, and so
they are part of the tetrapod group.

One step at a time

It might seem as though legs are just
too unlike fins, or that land animals are
nothing like fish, but remember: these
changes did not happen all at once. To
understand how the jigsaw fits together,
let's take a look at a few of the strange,
prehistoric creatures that fit somewhere
between "fish" and "tetrapod."

EUSTHENOPTERON

Pronounced: Yoos-then-op-ter-on
Lived: 385 MYA (Devonian)
Size: 6 feet (1.8 m) long

Eusthenopteron looked very like a fish, but it had some important differences.

The type of bones in the bases of the paired fins show the fins had strong muscles.

Typical fish-shaped body

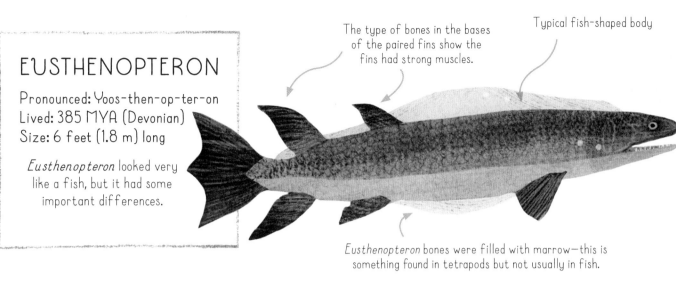

Eusthenopteron bones were filled with marrow—this is something found in tetrapods but not usually in fish.

Breathing holes on top of the head, and a strong ribcage, suggest *Tiktaalik* had lungs.

It had reduced gills at the back of the head, and had developed a neck.

TIKTAALIK

Pronounced: Tick-tall-ick
Lived: 375 MYA (Devonian)
Size: 8 feet (2.5 m) long

Tiktaalik is thought of by discoverers as neither fish nor tetrapod, but as a "fishopod."

Two pairs of muscular fins, below the body, were good for crawling.

Ichthyostega had lungs, although gills were still its main breathing organs.

A fish-like fin on the tail, like a modern newt, shows it spent most of its time in the water.

ICHTHYOSTEGA

Pronounced: Ick-thee-oh-steh-gah
Lived: 360 MYA (Devonian)
Size: 5 feet (1.5 m) long

Ichthyostega appeared even more like a land animal, but scientists think it still mostly lived in water.

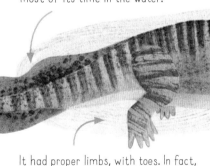

It had proper limbs, with toes. In fact, it had seven toes on the hind foot!

The joints of the front legs show that it could have dragged itself across land.

Why change?

Strangely enough, these changes did not make for an animal better fitted for life on land—rather, they helped it to live its life in shallow, weed-filled inland waters!

A NEW HOME

So, if the newt-like creatures we've just seen were adapted to live in shallow, weedy water, then what made them eventually crawl out onto land? What was it that drove the evolution of land-living tetrapods?

There are a number of possible reasons. Perhaps the shallow waters dried up occasionally and the inhabitants were forced to travel overland to find new water. Perhaps the other creatures living in shallow waters, such as giant water scorpions, became so dangerous that it was a good idea to seek a home elsewhere. Perhaps the newly evolving plant and insect life on land encouraged bigger animals to go out onto land to find food.

Whatever the reasons, the adaptations that made some animals better at living in shallow, weed-choked waters were a step toward to a land-living existence. Scientists call this "pre-adaptation." However, as you'll find out here, living on dry land means more than having lungs and legs!

Coping with gravity

Gravity was a problem. In water, an animal is buoyant. On land, it needs strong limbs to lift it clear of the ground, and a strong backbone to support the whole skeletal structure. These features are first seen in *Casineria.*

CASINERIA

Pronounced: Cass-een-eh-ria
Lived: 335 MYA (Carboniferous)
Size: 6 inches (15 cm) long

PEDERPES

Pronounced: Ped-er-peez
Lived: 350 MYA (Carboniferous)
Size: 3 ¼ feet (1 m) long

Forward march

To walk easily on land, an animal must have forward-facing feet, so that its toes can grip. *Pederpes* is the earliest known tetrapod to have forward-pointing feet. By this time the basic number of toes had become five—earlier animals like *Ichthyostega* and its relatives had seven or eight toes on each foot.

Eating their greens

With the flourishing array of land plants, it is hardly surprising that animals evolved to eat them. *Diadectes* was one of the first vegetarians. The sturdy pig-like body reflected the new complex digestive system that such a diet needed.

DIADECTES

Pronounced: Dy-a-dects
Lived: 290 MYA (Carboniferous)
Size: 10 feet (3 m) long

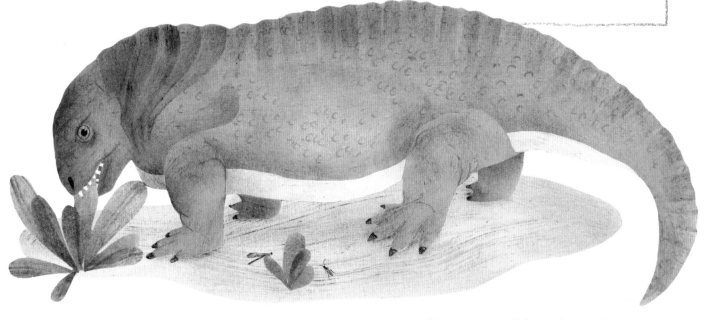

Eggs with shells

No matter how well-adapted they were to life on land, water-based vertebrates—like the amphibians—had to return to pools to lay their eggs. The next important step came with the evolution of eggs with hard, waterproof shells. These, in effect, carried their own pools with them, and could be laid on dry land. Lizard-like *Westlothiana* was one of the earliest creatures to lay this sort of egg.

WESTLOTHIANA

Pronounced: West-low-thee-anna
Lived: 330 MYA (Carboniferous)
Size: 12 inches (30 cm) long

In the right place at the right time

The lush, damp forests of the Carboniferous period were ideal for the animals that spent most of their lives in water. However, at the end of this period, widespread climate change wiped out many forests, and an ice age began. In this dryer and colder world, the animals that flourished were those that had already adapted to life on dry land.

WHEN LIZARDS WENT BACK TO THE WATER

By the Triassic period, a new type of animal had evolved. Was it a shark? A dolphin? No! In fact, it was neither. It had the same streamlined shape as both of these modern animals, with a fin on the back and a powerful tail. But this new animal was neither fish nor mammal. It was a reptile—an ichthyosaur.

Fish lizards

It was not long after the tetrapods appeared on land that some of them sought a return to the sea where their ancestors had evolved. The ichthyosaurs were the most successful of the animals to go back to the water. The name means "fish lizard."

Long, toothy jaws

Pointed snout

Limbs in the form of bony paddles, stiffened with gristle

CARTORHYNCHUS

Pronounced: Kar-toh-rink-us
Lived: 250 MYA (Early Triassic)
Size: 16 inches (40 cm) long

One of the earliest "fish lizards" to appear was a little animal called *Cartorhynchus*. Its body was streamlined, to slice its way through the water, and it had special limbs for swimming. These features were key to surviving in the sea. *Cartorhynchus* could probably flop around on a beach, like a seal. It may have been a stepping stone from land reptiles to ichthyosaurs.

CHAOHUSAURUS

Pronounced: Kay-oh-uh-sawr-us
Lived: 248 MYA (Early Triassic)
Size: 6 ½ feet (2 m) long

It did not take long for the classic ichthyosaur shape to appear, and *Chaohusaurus* was one of the first examples. Its streamlined body, pointed snout, flipper limbs, and finned tail were perfect for moving through the water, but they meant that it had lost all ability to live on land. Instead of coming ashore to lay eggs, it gave birth to live young in water.

SPECIAL LIMBS

Ichthyosaurs had paddles instead of hands. A human hand has 14 finger bones, but an ichthyosaur paddle may have had many more. An ichthyosaur's finger bones were fused together, which created a rigid support for the paddle.

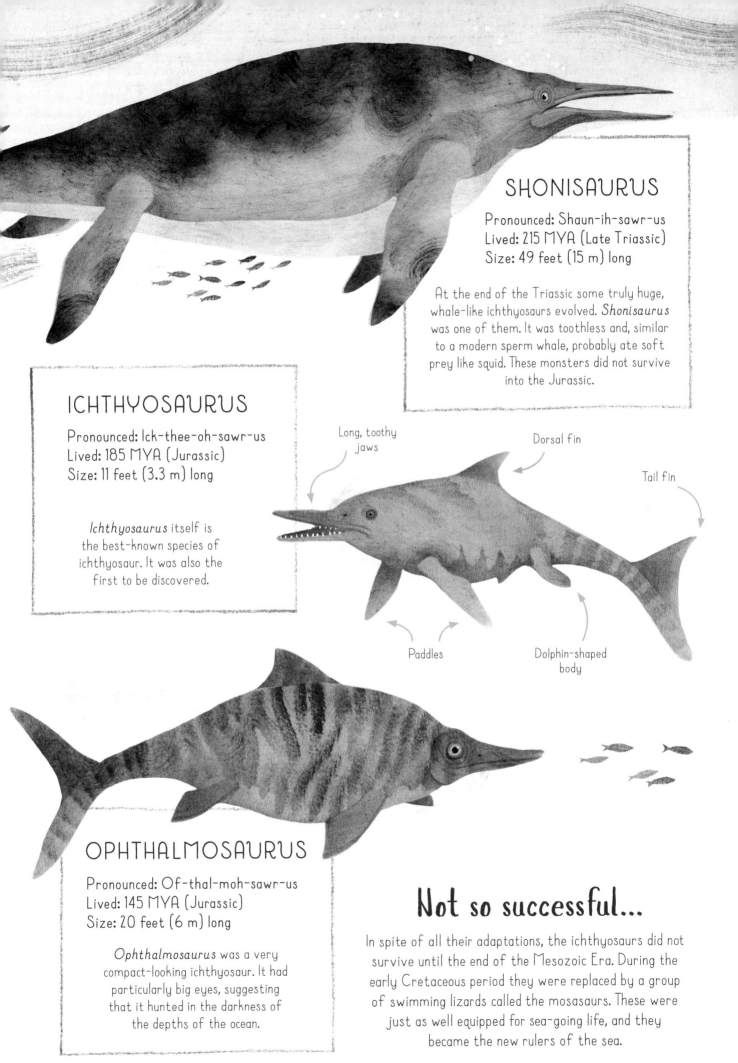

SHONISAURUS

Pronounced: Shaun-ih-sawr-us
Lived: 215 MYA (Late Triassic)
Size: 49 feet (15 m) long

At the end of the Triassic some truly huge, whale-like ichthyosaurs evolved. *Shonisaurus* was one of them. It was toothless and, similar to a modern sperm whale, probably ate soft prey like squid. These monsters did not survive into the Jurassic.

ICHTHYOSAURUS

Pronounced: Ick-thee-oh-sawr-us
Lived: 185 MYA (Jurassic)
Size: 11 feet (3.3 m) long

Ichthyosaurus itself is the best-known species of ichthyosaur. It was also the first to be discovered.

Long, toothy jaws

Dorsal fin

Tail fin

Paddles

Dolphin-shaped body

OPHTHALMOSAURUS

Pronounced: Of-thal-moh-sawr-us
Lived: 145 MYA (Jurassic)
Size: 20 feet (6 m) long

Ophthalmosaurus was a very compact-looking ichthyosaur. It had particularly big eyes, suggesting that it hunted in the darkness of the depths of the ocean.

Not so successful...

In spite of all their adaptations, the ichthyosaurs did not survive until the end of the Mesozoic Era. During the early Cretaceous period they were replaced by a group of swimming lizards called the mosasaurs. These were just as well equipped for sea-going life, and they became the new rulers of the sea.

SEA REPTILE SURVIVORS

The ichthyosaurs were not the only sea reptiles living at the time of the dinosaurs. The other main group was the plesiosaurs. Their ancestry goes back to about the time that the ichthyosaurs appeared. But unlike the ichthyosaurs, they survived until the end of the Cretaceous period.

CLAUDIOSAURUS

Pronounced: Klaw-di-oh-sawr-us
Lived: 250 MYA (Late Permian)
Size: 2 feet (60 cm) long

All the way back in Permian times, there was a small sea reptile which may have been related to the ancestors of the plesiosaurs. *Claudiosaurus* lived partly on land and partly in the water. It swam by smoothly swinging its long neck, body, and tail from side to side—just like a modern marine iguana.

Lightweight skeleton better suited to living in water than on land

Webbed feet for swimming

Long neck or big head?

Once the plesiosaur group was established, it split into two different lines. Each line then evolved in a different direction. The first group, called the elasmosaurs, had extremely long necks and tiny heads. The second group, called the pliosaurs, had short necks and very big heads.

PISTOSAURUS

Pronounced: Piss-toh-sore-us
Lived: 230 MYA (Middle Triassic)
Size: 10 feet (3 m) long

Scientists have no doubt that *Pistosaurus* was an ancestor of the plesiosaur group. It had a more rigid backbone than *Claudiosaurus*, so it had to swim by using its limbs rather than swinging its whole body. However, these limbs were paddles, not legs.

RHOMALEOSAURUS

Pronounced: Roh-mal-ee-oh-sawr-us
Lived: 185 MYA (Early Jurassic)
Size: 23 feet (7 m) long

Rhomaleosaurus was technically a pliosaur, but it seemed to fall between the two plesiosaur groups. It had a longish neck and a biggish head.

ELASMOSAURUS

Pronounced: Eh-laz-moh-sawr-us
Lived: 80 MYA (Late Cretaceous)
Size: 33 feet (10 m) long

The most spectacular of the elasmosaurs was *Elasmosaurus* itself. It swam the Cretaceous oceans and shallow seas by using its paddles in a "flying" action, like a modern penguin. It darted at fish with its extremely long neck— 72 vertebrae long!

LIOPLEURODON

Pronounced: Lee-oh-plur-oh-don
Lived: 145 MYA (Late Jurassic)
Size: 20 feet (6 m) long

Liopleurodon was a typical pliosaur, with an enormous toothy head connected to the body by a very short neck—a bit like a modern sperm whale. Its powerful paddles were ideal for sudden bursts of speed as it attacked the other big sea reptiles on which it fed.

A sea of monsters

Imagine what it must have been like in the prehistoric oceans, with toothy reptiles swimming through the murky depths. Some were small, but others were giants. Luckily for us, these fearsome predators died out millions of years before humans appeared. But some of them look very much like the sea monsters that sailors and artists have imagined over the years!

WHEN REPTILES GREW WINGS

When we look at any illustration of a dinosaur landscape, we always see winged shapes wheeling about in the sky. They are as much a part of that environment as the dinosaurs themselves. But these winged creatures are not birds. They are the flying reptiles—the pterosaurs.

We have found fossils of many different sorts of pterosaurs, and we know how they evolved once they appeared. However, there is one thing that we must admit to not knowing. The big mystery is, from what did they evolve?

Tracing the family tree

We do know that pterosaurs were distantly related to the dinosaurs, but how distant? Just who were their immediate ancestors? There are two possibilities.

The first is that their ancestors are to be found among the dinosauromorphs. These are the closest ancestors of the dinosaurs. Late Triassic *Scleromochlus*, about 8 inches (20 cm) long, is a good example. Recent research suggests that it could jump like a kangaroo. Perhaps this was an early stage on the way to flight?

Scleromochlus's kangaroo-like legs may have helped it jump high to catch flying insects.

The other possibility is that the ancestor was further back in the evolutionary line, in a group we call the archosauromorphs. These are the more remote ancestors of the dinosaurs but also of the crocodiles and all sorts of other beasts that existed during the age of the dinosaurs. They were a long way from evolving into flying creatures, though!

20-inch (50-centimetre)-long early Triassic *Prolacerta* is a good example of an archosasauromorph.

A FALSE TRAIL

Scientists used to think that the Triassic gliding reptile *Sharovipteryx* may have been an ancestor of the pterosaurs, but they don't think so now. The only shared feature is the gliding membrane between the hind legs. This would have allowed *Sharovipteryx* to glide but not fly, and it is no more similar to the pterosaurs than many other gliding reptiles of the time.

Into the air

Whatever their ancestors, the pterosaurs suddenly appeared in the late Triassic. The early types, a group known as the rhamphorhynchoids, all had narrow wings, a long tail, a short neck, and short wrist bones.

RHAMPHORHYNCHUS

Pronounced: Ran-for-ink-us
Lived: 150 MYA (Late Jurassic)
Size: 6 foot (1.8 m) wingspan

Rhamphorhynchus is a good example of a rhamphorhynchoid pterosaur. Its needle-like teeth suggest it probably caught fish.

Toward the end of the Jurassic period one of the rhamphorhynchoid families gave rise to the pterodactyloids. Unlike the earlier types, these had broad wings, a short tail, a long neck, and long wrist bones. These pterodactyloids replaced the earlier forms, took over the skies, and survived until the end of the age of dinosaurs.

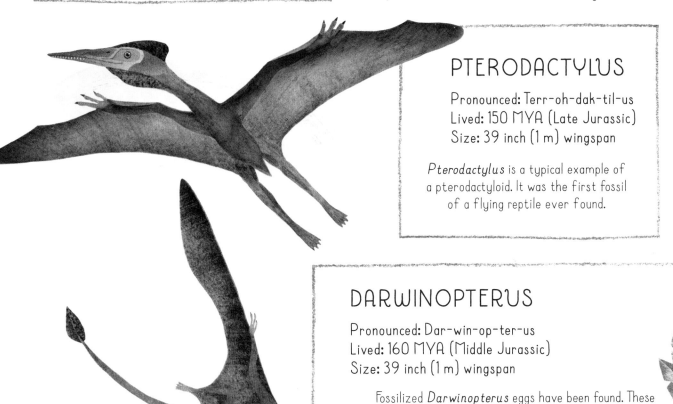

PTERODACTYLUS

Pronounced: Terr-oh-dak-til-us
Lived: 150 MYA (Late Jurassic)
Size: 39 inch (1 m) wingspan

Pterodactylus is a typical example of a pterodactyloid. It was the first fossil of a flying reptile ever found.

DARWINOPTERUS

Pronounced: Dar-win-op-ter-us
Lived: 160 MYA (Middle Jurassic)
Size: 39 inch (1 m) wingspan

Fossilized *Darwinopterus* eggs have been found. These show that pterosaur eggshells were soft and leathery, like those of snakes and crocodiles, not hard like those of birds and dinosaurs.

But how do we know?

Scientists can tell that the rhamphorhynchoids evolved into pterodactyloids because they have found fossils of a pterosaur that shows features of both. This is what is known as a "transitional form". The pterosaur, *Darwinopterus*, lived during the middle Jurassic period. It had the body, tail, and wings of a rhamphorhynchoid, but the long neck and head of a pterodactyloid.

MASTERS OF ALL THE SKIES

Look at the birds that fly around us today—all the different kinds.
There are little insect-eating birds, with tiny pointed beaks. There are big
fruit-eating birds with strong nutcracking beaks. There are filter-feeding birds
with sieve-like beaks. There are seabirds with long beaks for catching fish.

It was the same with the pterodactyloids. Once their basic shape
had evolved at the end of the Jurassic, all sorts of head shapes
developed for all sorts of lifestyles. Let's look at a few of them.

PTERODACTYLUS

The head of *Pterodactylus* itself
shows the basic shape. The long
jaws and the sharp teeth at the
front make it ideal for catching and
eating a range of foods, such as
lizards, insects, and fish.

TROPEOGNATHUS

Tropeognathus had long needle-
like teeth for gripping slippery
prey, and vanes on the jaw tips
for cleaving through water.
It was a fish-hunter.

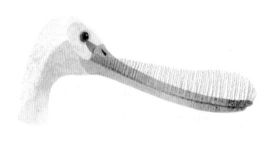

TAPEJARA

The short, strong jaws of
crested *Tapejara* were
perfect for eating fruit
and other plant material.

PTERODAUSTRO

The bristles in the long, narrow
jaws of *Pterodaustro* show
that it fed by filtering tiny
animals out of shallow water,
as the modern flamingo does.

NYCTOSAURUS

Have you noticed how many of the
pterodactyloids had big head crests?
Perhaps the strangest of these was
toothless *Nyctosaurus*. We have no
idea what this crest was used for.
It may have supported a sail as big
as one of its wings, but again we do
not know. What a mystery!

What made pterodactyloids such successful fliers?

Well, their wings were not just simple webs of skin, but contained air sacs. These gave the wings an aerodynamic cross-section, like the wings of an airplane. The sacs also helped their breathing, allowing these warm-blooded creatures to get all the oxygen they needed. Cold-blooded reptiles can't move quickly enough to fly.

Like a giraffe, *Quetzalcoatlus's* long, stiff neck allowed its head to reach down to feed.

Quetzalcoatlus (pronounced Kwet-zal-koh-at-lus) lived in inland areas 70 MYA, during the Cretaceous period.

Monsters on the ground

These creatures didn't just rule the skies. Some of the biggest pterodactyloids, such as *Quetzalcoatlus*, were so big they stood as high as modern giraffes. They may have spent most of their time on the ground. We know that pterosaurs stood like this from their fossilised footprints. These show impressions of flat-footed, four-toed hind feet, and two- to three-fingered forefeet with a sweep of the wing off to the side. While on the ground, monstrous *Quetzalcoatlus* may have hunted small dinosaurs.

Outstretched, *Quetzalcoatlus* had a wingspan of around 36 feet (11 m).

WHEN CROCODILES RULED THE WORLD

The cold-blooded crocodile lies in the mud, camouflaged as a log. For long periods it is motionless, saving its energy. Then an unsuspecting antelope comes close to the water's edge. Suddenly, with a vast burst of energy, the crocodile leaps out of the water, seizes the antelope, and drags it beneath the surface. Afterward, the crocodile can go back to its sluggish ways, eating the prize at its leisure.

It is often said that crocodiles have remained unchanged since the days of the dinosaurs, so you might think that crocodiles have only ever been cold-blooded water dwellers. In fact, the real story is much more interesting.

The crocodile family was around long before the dinosaurs and occupied every niche, from little insect-eaters to huge hunters. Powerful, active, and warm-blooded, the crocodile family were the rulers of the world for about 50 million years until the dinosaurs took over.

HESPEROSUCHUS

Pronounced: Hess-per-oh-sook-us
Lived: 220 MYA (Late Triassic)
Size: 5 feet (1.5 m) long

Scampering little *Hesperosuchus* was a distant ancestor of the crocodiles. It was a fast hunter, probably preying on little lizards or even insects in the oases of the northern continents during the Triassic period.

CARNUFEX

Pronounced: Car-nu-fex
Lived: 230 MYA (Late Triassic)
Size: 10 feet (3 m) long

A sharp-toothed, meat-eating hunter that could stand on its hind legs, *Carnufex* could have been mistaken for a dinosaur. However, fossils reveal that its hip joints were totally wrong for a dinosaur, and the structure of the skull show it to have been a member of the crocodile family.

SAUROSUCHUS

Pronounced: Sawr-oh-sook-us
Lived: 230 MYA (Late Triassic)
Size: 23 feet (7 m) long

Saurosuchus was the biggest meat-eater of
the time. The earliest dinosaurs were around as
well, but they would have avoided it. This mighty
creature was the lion of the Triassic period: it
prowled around the ferny riverside forests,
hunting big, plant-eating reptiles.

STAGONOLEPIS

Pronounced: Stag-ono-leh-piss
Lived: 220 MYA (Late Triassic)
Size: 10 feet (3 m) long

Not all ancient crocs ate meat. Some,
such as *Stagonolepis*, had evolved to
be vegetarian. With its heavy body and
pig-like head and snout, *Stagonolepis*
tore up the sparse plants that
were scattered across
the late Triassic deserts
of the northern continents.

DESMATOSUCHUS

Pronounced: Dez-mat-oh-sook-us
Lived: 220 MYA (Late Triassic)
Size: 16 ½ feet (5 m) long

Desmatosuchus, a
relative and herd-living
neighbor of *Stagonolepis*, had armor plates across
its back as its cousin had, but also had spines
sticking out of the sides and shoulders.
It needed these for defense against the
meat-eating types of early crocodiles.

Warm-blooded legacy

Of all the different types of early crocodile, it was the slow-moving, semi-aquatic
predator lifestyle that survived until the present day. But when we look closely
at a modern croc, there are clues to its complicated history.

If we look at the bones of a modern crocodile's ankle we can see that its ancestors once walked on
land full time. Even though it is cold-blooded, a crocodile's heart is the heart of a warm-blooded
animal. This must be a leftover from when its ancestors were warm-blooded like birds
and mammals. So you see, there is more to crocodiles than meets the eye!

A CROC FOR EVERY HABITAT

All was going well for the crocodiles, but then the dinosaurs evolved.
The reign of the crocodiles was over!

But this does not mean that the crocodiles disappeared: instead, they became adapted to niches that the dinosaurs did not occupy. During the age of the dinosaurs, the warm-blooded crocodile relatives could be found wallowing in swamps, burrowing in the ground, and even swimming in oceans.

GEOSAURUS

Pronounced: Jee-oh-sawr-us
Lived: 145 MYA (Late Jurassic)
Size: 10 feet (3 m) long

Like the ichthyosaurs (see pages 16-19), which lived during the same period, *Geosaurus* was so well-adapted to sea life that it had paddles instead of legs, and a fish-like fin on the tail. All sorts of new fish and squid-like animals appeared in the oceans at the beginning of the Jurassic period, and *Geosaurus* and others evolved to hunt them. Although there were many sea-living reptiles at the time, the dinosaurs themselves did not venture out into the oceans.

ANATOSUCHUS

Pronounced: A-nat-oh-sook-us
Lived: 115 MYA (Early Cretaceous)
Size: 28 inches (70 cm) long

With a broad, duck-like beak, *Anatosuchus* waded in shallow ponds and streams scooping out little mud-dwelling creatures, just as many types of modern duck do. Its splayed toes and long legs may have helped it to walk through squelchy mud.

ARMADILLOSUCHUS

Pronounced: Arm-a-dill-oh-sook-us
Lived: 80 MYA (Late Cretaceous)
Size: 6 ½ feet (2 m) long

South American burrowing
Armadillosuchus had armor similar
to a modern armadillo's. The jaws show
that it could chew its food like mammals do,
and its teeth were capable of dealing with meat,
insects, roots, and all sorts of other things.

SIMOSUCHUS

Pronounced: Si-moh-sook-us
Lived: 70 MYA (Late Cretaceous)
Size: 30 inches (75 cm) long

With its pug-nose, its plump body, its long legs, and
its short tail, *Simosuchus* did not look much like a
crocodile at all. It lived in Madagascar and its head and
body shape tell us it must have been an herbivore.

SARCOSUCHUS

Pronounced: Sar-koh-such-us
Lived: 100 MYA (Cretaceous)
Size: 39 feet (12 m) long

Sarcosuchus was a monster of a beast, big
enough to catch and eat dinosaurs. Aside
from its huge size, though, it probably looks
very familiar to you. *Sarcosuchus* fossils
are evidence that the shape and lifestyle
of the modern crocodile—the cold-blooded,
slow-moving, semi-aquatic ambush
predator—was well established
during the time of
the dinosaurs.

WHEN SNAKES HAD LEGS

Snakes are rather strange creatures. Scientists put them in a group called the tetrapods, meaning "four feet." But snakes do not have four feet—they have no feet at all!

There are many stories that try to explain what happened to snakes' legs. The Ancient Greeks said that Poseidon, god of the sea, watched an animal that was too lazy to use its legs on land. He commanded the tiger to chew its legs off in punishment for its laziness. Of course, the truth is a bit more complicated than that.

What happened to the legs?

We can tell from studying their genes that snakes and lizards are closely related. The ancestors of snakes were part of the lizard family, and they were four-footed. Today's snakes have a gene that prevents legs from growing. But a snake's long, legless body is hardly a punishment. It is the ideal shape for certain lifestyles, particularly swimming and burrowing.

LEG LEFTOVERS

Modern pythons have bits of leg and hip bones remaining in their skeleton. You can see them at the lower end of the ribcage. This is evidence that their ancestors had legs.

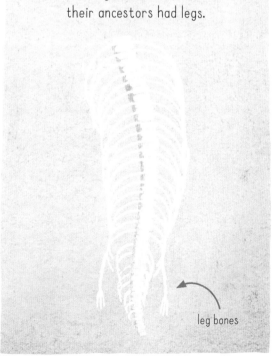

leg bones

TETRAPODOPHIS

Pronounced: Tet-ra-pod-oh-fiss
Lived: 150 MYA (Early Cretaceous)
Size: 6 inches (15 cm) long

Tetrapodophis, from Brazil, seems to have been a snake, but it had two pairs of tiny legs. Some scientists think that it may not have been a snake at all, but a member of a related group.

A very well-adapted animal

It is not just leglessness that makes snakes unusual. Their eyelids are transparent and permanently closed, offering protection against soil particles while burrowing. Snakes have only one functioning lung—easier to fit into the long, narrow body. Their skeleton has more vertebrae and ribs than other tetrapods, allowing agile, sinuous movement. As they have no claws, they have evolved other ways of killing their prey—either by poison or by squeezing.

PACHYRHACHIS

Pronounced: Pak-hee-rah-kiss
Lived: 95 MYA (Late Cretaceous)
Size: 39 inches (1 m) long

Pachyrhachis was a swimming snake from Israel. It still had a pair of hind legs. The strength of its bones and ribs suggests that it swam and hunted in the ocean, like a modern sea snake.

TITANOBOA

Pronounced: Ty-tan-oh-bo-ah
Lived: 60 MYA (Palaeocene)
Size: 43 feet (13 m) long

The enormous *Titanoboa*, from Colombia, is an example of the legless body shape that has been with us ever since Cretaceous times. *Titanoboa* lived after the extinction of the dinosaurs but before the big mammals evolved, so we are not sure what this monster actually ate. It may have hunted the very large crocodiles that lived in its steamy, tropical home.

NAJASH

Pronounced: Na-jash
Lived: 95 MYA (Late Cretaceous)
Size: 6 ½ feet (2 m) long

Another snake with hind legs was *Najash*, from Argentina. Its legs were so small that it is difficult to imagine their purpose. *Najash* seems to have been a burrowing snake.

WHEN BIRDS HAD TEETH

Birds! They're chirpy little feathery creatures, singers of melodious songs and masters of flight. It's difficult to grasp the fact that their remote ancestors were fierce meat-eating dinosaurs, but it is true. And if we look at the fossils of the birds that existed at the time of the dinosaurs, we can see how they changed—arms became wings, and jaws became beaks.

A halfway stage

For more than 150 years we have known that birds are descended from dinosaurs. That was when quarrymen in Germany found fossils of *Archaeopteryx*—an animal that seemed to be half dinosaur and half bird. Let's look at a typical small, meat-eating dinosaur and a modern bird, and compare their features to those of *Archaeopteryx*.

Jaws and teeth

Clawed hands

Long, bony tail

SINOSAUROPTERYX

Pronounced: Sy-noh-sawr-op-ter-ix
Lived: 130 MYA (Early Cretaceous)
Size: 43 inches (1.1 m) long

Sinosauropteryx was a speedy runner. Fossil remains of its stomach show that it ate small lizards and mammals. It was the first dinosaur found with feathers, though we now know that many dinosaurs shared this feature.

Lightweight beak without teeth

Wings instead of hands

No bones in the tail— just feathers

PARROT

Lives: 20 MYA-present day
Size: varies by species

Unlike the dinosaurs before them, modern birds such as the parrot have evolved a body shape that allows flight, and have lost the front claws, teeth, and bony tail of their ancestors.

Jaws and teeth

Wings but with claws

Long, bony tail covered with feathers

ARCHAEOPTERYX

Pronounced: Ar-key-op-ter-ix
Lived: 150 MYA (Late Jurassic)
Size: 20 inches (50 cm) long

Archaeopteryx is one of the most important and exciting fossil discoveries, because its mix of features revealed for the first time that dinosaurs evolved into birds. The word *Archaeopteryx* means "ancient wing".

Dinosaur or bird?

All these changes did not happen at once. Little changes, like the loss of teeth, or the development of long feathers, allowed their owners to find food and move about in the trees more easily. Eventually all the changes combined to produce an animal that was lightweight enough to be able to fly—and so birds as we know them emerged.

You might think that dinosaurs died out 65 million years ago. In fact, the boundary between what we call dinosaurs and what we call birds is so vague that many paleontologists think that birds should still be called dinosaurs!

So dinosaurs changed into birds and flew away...but why?

BIRD PARTS—BIT BY BIT

The features that make birds recognizable as birds did not all appear at once. Neither did they appear specifically to allow birds to fly. Each feature— feathers, a lightweight beak, loss of a heavy tail, and so on—developed time and time again in different dinosaurs. Eventually, a combination of these led to the flying creatures that we know today.

Warm-blooded

During the Cretaceous period, toward the end of the age of dinosaurs, some small meat-eating dinosaurs evolved features that we would expect to see on birds. These dinosaurs were already covered in feathers. This shows that they were warm-blooded and used to an active lifestyle.

EPIDEXIPTERYX

Pronounced: Epi-dex-ip-teh-rix
Lived: 164 MYA (Late Jurassic)
Size: 10 inches (25 cm) long

About the size of a pigeon, *Epidexipteryx* had a stubby tail and long tail feathers.

CAUDIPTERYX

Pronounced: Caw-dip-teh-rix
Lived: 125 MYA (Early Cretaceous)
Size: 39 inches (1 m) long

Flightless *Caudipteryx* was a bit like a long-legged turkey. It had long display feathers on the arms and the tail, and teeth in its short jaws.

CONFUCIUSORNIS

Pronounced: Con-few-shuss-or-nis
Lived: 160 MYA (Late Jurassic)
Size: 10 inches (25 cm) long

Confuciusornis was the size of
a crow and had long tail feathers,
proper wings, a beak—and it could fly.
But it still had claws on its wings.

YANORNIS

Pronounced: Yan-or-nis
Lived: 125 MYA
        (Early Cretaceous)
Size: 12 inches (30 cm) long

Chicken-sized *Yanornis* was almost
completely like a modern bird, except
it still had small teeth.

Feathers without flight

All of these dinosaurs had feathers, but they weren't originally used for
flight. Short feathers were for warmth, long feathers on the wings and
tail were for showing off to mates and to enemies. Only some of these
animals were light enough to fly. All these different types, flying or
not, lived in different places—some in trees and some on the ground.

Disaster strikes

At the end of the Cretaceous period, an asteroid hit Earth. Shock waves, fires, and
tsunamis produced instant disasters. Long-lasting climate change made vast areas of the
world uninhabitable. The event wiped out much of the life on Earth, including all the dinosaurs
and most of the new bird types. So which were the few lucky birds that survived, and why?

BIRDS RECOVER...AND THRIVE!

What a mess Earth was in after the asteroid struck! All the forests had burned down. All the tree-living animals, including the birds, were gone.

But not all life was destroyed. The survivors were mostly small animals that were not too specialized for any particular food or lifestyle. Such little animals found shelter during the greatest disruptions, and survived on the small amount of food there was to be found.

It looks as if the birds that survived were small, unspecialized types like these that lived on the ground rather than in trees.

Walking survivor

One of the earliest birds known from the Palaeogene period, after the asteroid impact, was *Foro*. It had long legs showing that it was a ground-living, rather than a tree-living bird.

The damage from the impact wiped out all the tree cover on the planet. It was about 1.4 million years before forests began to recover. When they did, ground-living birds like *Foro* evolved into perching tree-dwellers once more, as well as all the other types with their different lifestyles.

FORO

Pronounced: For-oh
Lived: 48 MYA (Eocene)
Size: 24 inches (60 cm) long

COPEPTERYX

Pronounced: Cop-epp-teh-rix
Lived: 28 MYA (Oligocene)
Size: 6 ½ feet (2 m) long

With *Copepteryx*, the wings became paddles, and the bird adopted a swimming rather than a flying lifestyle, like the modern penguin.

NEOCATHARTES

Pronounced: Nee-oh-kath-ar-teez
Lived: 37 MYA (Eocene)
Size: 39 inch (1 m) wingspan

The scavenging vulture
lifestyle appeared with
Neocathartes, which looked
like a long-legged vulture.

PENGANA

Pronounced: Pen-gan-na
Lived: 23 MYA (Miocene)
Size: 6 foot (1.8 m) wingspan

Pengana was a bird
of prey very similar
to modern hawks.

Variety of life

Over millions of years, birds have evolved into so many
different forms. Think of all the wonderful birds we see
around us today—the seed-eaters, the insect-hunters, the
great eagles, the tiny hummingbirds, the brilliant peacocks—
even the huge flightless ostriches and emus. Their distant
ancestors were the great meat-eating dinosaurs.

QUASISYNDACTYLUS

Pronounced: Kwah-zee-sin-dak-till-us
Lived: 48 MYA (Eocene)
Size: 7 inches (18 cm) long

Tiny *Quasisyndactylus* lived on
fish like the modern kingfisher.

PRESBYORNIS

Pronounced: Prez-bi-or-nis
Lived: 50 MYA (Eocene)
Size: 18 inches (45 cm) tall

Presbyornis was a
wading bird, a bit like a
modern duck but shaped
more like a flamingo.

WHEN WHALES WALKED ON LAND

The whale! The biggest animal on our planet. Heart that weighs a ton. Arteries that you could swim through. Tongue as heavy as an elephant. Swallowing forty million little sea creatures a day! But whales of that size have only been around for about the past two million years. Fifty million years ago, their ancestors looked very different indeed...

The whales that did not look like whales

We'll begin our journey in the Eocene period 50 million years ago, with a little cat-sized animal, scampering along the ferny bank of a tropical river in what is now Pakistan. It is called *Indohyus* and it belongs to the group that evolved into the whales. At that time, the area was made up of swamps, deltas, and lagoons and, for the next few million years, most of the whale's ancestors lived here. Let's meet four of the earliest whale ancestors, which hardly looked like whales at all.

We know that it is related to whales because of the shape of the ear bones.

INDOHYUS

Pronounced: In-doh-hi-us
Lived 48 MYA (Eocene)
Size: 32 inches (80 cm) long

Indohyus's slender leg bones were quite heavy, suggesting that it spent some time in the water. Scientists think that it used the water to escape predators, like the modern mouse-deer which forages along the African riverbanks, and plunges into the water to escape birds of prey.

Its teeth show us that *Indohyus* was a plant-eater.

PAKICETUS

Pronounced: Pah-kee-see-tuss
Lived: 50 MYA (Eocene)
Size: 6 ½ feet (2 m) long

Pakicetus was another amphibious animal, spending time in water and on land. Chemicals in the fossil bones show that it wallowed in freshwater, and ate land animals and plants.

Eyes were like a crocodile's—on top of the skull so that it could see above the water while its body was submerged.

Its teeth show that *Pakicetus* was a meat-eater.

Its jaws show that it could feed underwater, hunting swimming animals and fish.

It had strong hind legs and a muscular tail, meaning it swam like a modern otter.

AMBULOCETUS

Pronounced: Am-bew-lo-see-tuss
Lived: 49 MYA (Eocene)
Size: 10 feet (3 m) long

Ambulocetus lived mostly in water, like a crocodile. Bone chemistry shows that it lived in both freshwater and saltwater. It may still have had fur like its ancestors, or it may have had bare skin like later aquatic mammals, but there is no evidence one way or another.

Its feet were broad and possibly webbed.

REMINGTONOCETUS

Pronounced: Rem-ing-ton-oh-see-tuss
Lived: 45 MYA (Eocene)
Size: 10 feet (3 m) long

By the time crocodile-shaped *Remingtonocetus* had evolved, these ancestral whales lived almost full time in the sea. Its whale-like ear had lost the structures that are important for maintaining balance on land, showing that it must have spent most of its time in the sea.

It was a cunning hunter, using its sense of smell to catch fish.

As with *Ambulocetus*, we cannot tell whether or not it had fur.

Its fossils have been found in shallow lagoon deposits.

Even this creature still doesn't look much like a whale...

37

THE WHALE SHAPE EVOLVES

Soon, whales became completely seagoing. They did not need to live on land, and so they lost the ability to walk. Their weight-bearing legs disappeared, becoming fins and paddles instead. Their bodies became streamlined, allowing them to move quickly through the water. They began to look a bit more like the whales we know today.

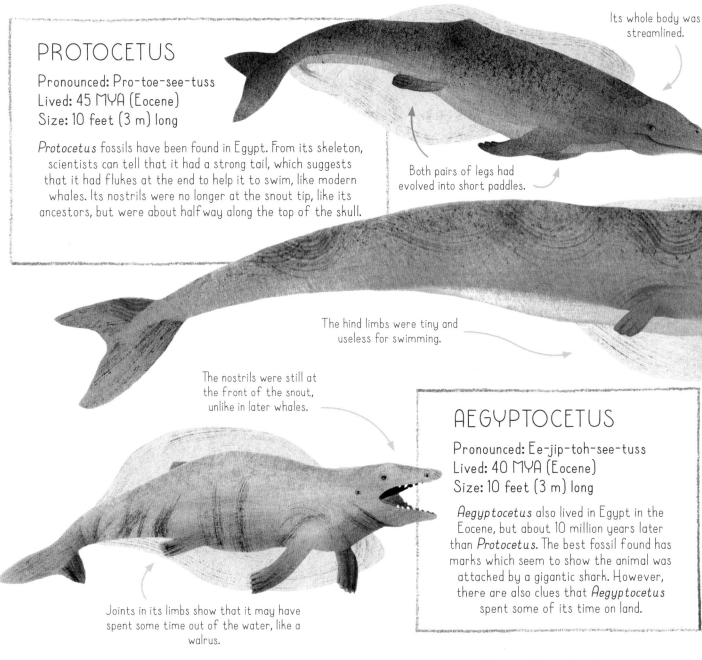

PROTOCETUS

Pronounced: Pro-toe-see-tuss
Lived: 45 MYA (Eocene)
Size: 10 feet (3 m) long

Protocetus fossils have been found in Egypt. From its skeleton, scientists can tell that it had a strong tail, which suggests that it had flukes at the end to help it to swim, like modern whales. Its nostrils were no longer at the snout tip, like its ancestors, but were about halfway along the top of the skull.

Its whole body was streamlined.

Both pairs of legs had evolved into short paddles.

The hind limbs were tiny and useless for swimming.

The nostrils were still at the front of the snout, unlike in later whales.

AEGYPTOCETUS

Pronounced: Ee-jip-toh-see-tuss
Lived: 40 MYA (Eocene)
Size: 10 feet (3 m) long

Aegyptocetus also lived in Egypt in the Eocene, but about 10 million years later than *Protocetus*. The best fossil found has marks which seem to show the animal was attacked by a gigantic shark. However, there are also clues that *Aegyptocetus* spent some of its time on land.

Joints in its limbs show that it may have spent some time out of the water, like a walrus.

SPOT THE NOSTRIL!

The nostrils of the first whales were at the tip of the snout, the same as in modern dogs, deer, and many other land mammals.

In later whales, nostrils were farther back, to help the animal to breathe at the water's surface.

In modern whales, nostrils are at the top of the skull, forming the blowhole.

BASILOSAURUS

Pronounced: Ba-sill-oh-sawr-us
Lived: 35 MYA (Eocene)
Size: 59 feet (18 m) long

Basilosaurus was a bit of an oddity. It was huge in comparison with other early whales. The big whales that we know today did not evolve until many millions of years later. Don't be confused by the name, though. *Basilosaurus* was not a dinosaur! The first person to discover it thought that it was, and gave it a misleading name. Fossils have been found all over the world, showing that these whales lived in the open ocean.

It had a long and narrow body, like a mythical sea serpent.

It had front paddles only, and they still had an elbow joint like a modern seal.

DORUDON

Pronounced: Dor-uh-don
Lived: 35 MYA (Eocene)
Size: 16 ½ feet (5 m) long

Dorudon was a small relative of *Basilosaurus*, living in the same areas at the same time. It was only 16 ½ feet (5 meters) long, but was so much like *Basilosaurus* that when it was first discovered, scientists thought it was a baby.

Its body shape was much less sea serpent-like than *Basilosaurus*.

Unlike modern whales, it still had small flippers where back legs once were.

The tale is in the teeth

The four animals shown here belong to a group known as the archaeocetes—the "ancient whales." Their teeth were very distinctive. Usually they had sharp teeth at the front of the jaw, for grabbing prey, and deep-rooted, triangular saw-edged teeth at the back, for tearing it up. They fed on sea animals and fish that were smaller than they were. Damage to their fossil bones show that they were preyed upon by giant sharks. But, as whale evolution continued, all that was about to change.

MODERN WHALES APPEAR

There are two types of modern whale: the baleen whales and the toothed whales. These two types separated about 30 million years ago.

The baleen whales are the big ones. They have no teeth but feed by sieving out small creatures, called krill, from the ocean water. For this they use gristly plates called baleen in their mouths. They take vast mouthfuls of seawater and push it out through the baleen using their huge tongue, keeping the krill inside.

Toothed whales are generally smaller, and they feed on squid and fish that they catch with their teeth. Unlike the teeth of their ancestors, the teeth of modern toothed whales are usually all the same size and same shape. Dolphins and other small whales are part of this group. As we follow the whale ancestor's journey into the present day, we are going to focus on the baleen whales.

AETIOCETUS

Pronounced: Ee-tee-oh-see-tuss
Lived: 25 MYA (Oligocene)
Size: 13 feet (4 m) long

Aetiocetus was not the direct ancestor of baleen whales—true baleen whales also existed during the Oligocene. However *Aetiocetus* is particularly interesting because it had both teeth and baleen in its mouth, showing it must be close to the ancestors of both the toothed whale and baleen whale lines.

The baleen did not fossilize, but we know it was there because of the holes in the upper jaw bone where it grew.

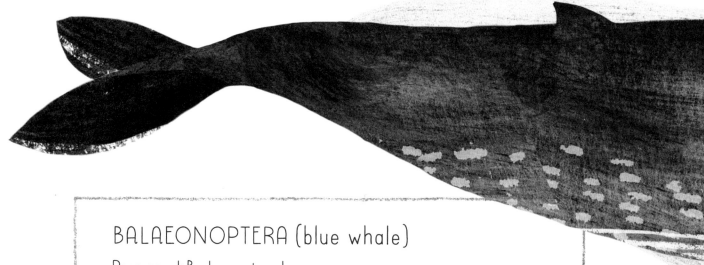

BALAEONOPTERA (blue whale)

Pronounced: Ba-len-op-ter-ah
Lives: 2 MYA-present day
Size: 82 feet (25 m) long

Balaeonoptera is regarded as the biggest vertebrate that ever lived. Giant whales such as this only evolved about 2 million years ago.

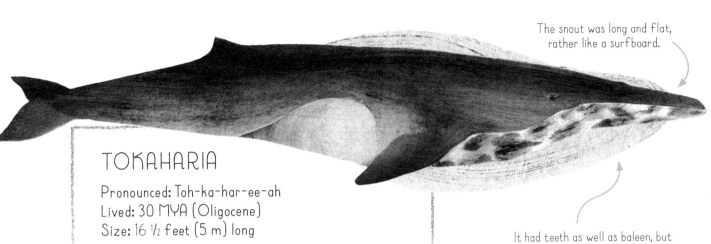

The snout was long and flat, rather like a surfboard.

TOKAHARIA

Pronounced: Toh-ka-har-ee-ah
Lived: 30 MYA (Oligocene)
Size: 16 ½ feet (5 m) long

Tokaharia fossils have been found in New Zealand. Chemicals in the bones show that it migrated north and south in the Southern Ocean, as modern whales do. It is the earliest known whale that definitely had baleen.

It had teeth as well as baleen, but they were tiny and do not seem to have had any function.

It had large front flippers, but no hind limbs.

Rise of the giants

About two million years ago, the baleen whales suddenly became huge. Until then they had been prey to a 59-foot (18 m)-long giant shark called *Megalodon*. Once they had evolved to a huge size, *Megalodon* could not hunt them anymore. Meanwhile, toothed whales evolved echolocation (a way of "seeing" by listening to echoes), and they used this to avoid the *Megalodon* attacks. Deprived of its main prey, the *Megalodon* shark finally went extinct, and baleen whales became the giants of the ocean.

The fluted surface beneath the chin allows the mouth to expand as it fills with water while hunting krill.

It hunts krill by smell, whereas toothed whales hunt their prey by echolocation.

WHEN RHINOS GREW HUGE

Think of a rhinoceros and what do you picture? A big, solid animal with horns and short, strong legs. It lumbers around the plains, grazing on grasses and other plants. Scientists have found fossils of many similar animals, dating back millions of years. Yet although these animals looked similar, none of them were actually related! How can this be?

ARSINOITHERIUM

Pronounced: Ar-sin-oy-theer-ee-um
Lived: 30 MYA (Oligocene)
Size: 10 feet (3 m) long

Arsinoitherium, found in North Africa, looked like a rhino, but with double the number of horns. It had two small horns and two massive ones. However, it was more closely related to the elephant and the manatee than to the rhinoceros.

Same, but different

Thanks to evolution, over many generations an animal's shape gradually changes. It becomes better suited to its lifestyle and environment. Today's rhinos have bodies that are perfect for their diet and habitat. And it is evidently a shape that ticks a lot of boxes, because throughout history it has evolved in many unrelated animal families. This is called "convergent evolution." The same process is the reason that ichthyosaurs, sharks, and dolphins have similar-shaped bodies, even though they are not related.

HYRACHYUS

Pronounced: Hi-ra-kee-us
Lived: 48 MYA (Palaeocene)
Size: 59 inches (1.5 m) long

The earliest rhinoceros relative that we know of looked very different. *Hyrachyus* was a dog-sized animal that scampered around, browsing on leaves in jungle undergrowth in Europe and North America. It was probably the ancestor of the tapir, as well as the rhinoceros.

HYRACODON

Pronounced: Hi-ra-koh-don
Lived: 32 MYA (Oligocene)
Size: 59 inches (1.5 m) long

A later inhabitant of North America, *Hyracodon* looked a bit like *Hyrachyus*, but it grazed on grass rather than eating leaves. It ran around on slender legs with three-toed feet.

Changing with the times

As time went on, the landscape changed. About 35 million years ago, forests gave way to open grasslands, and different-shaped animals fitted the new conditions better. On open grassland, there was no place to hide. An animal with long legs and lightweight feet, like *Hyracodon*, could escape hunting animals by running away. On the other hand, large animals with a huge body mass and intimidating size would make any predator think twice. The rhinoceroses mostly evolved to be larger. Horns developed as very visible display structures, for signaling to mates, or as warnings to enemies, and later these were found to be useful as weapons, too.

TRIGONIAS

Pronounced: Tri-goh-nee-us
Lived: 35 MYA (Eocene)
Size: 7 feet (2.1 m) long

Trigonias was twice the size of *Hyrachyus* and looked very much like a modern rhinoceros. The main differences were that it had no horn, and five toes instead of the three of the modern rhino. It lived on the plains of North America.

PARACERATHERIUM

Pronounced: Para-sera-theer-ee-un
Lived: 28 MYA (Oligocene)
Size: 26 feet (8 m) long, 16 feet (4.8 m) high at the shoulder

Paraceratherium was probably the biggest land mammal that ever existed. Living in Europe and Asia, it was a hornless rhinoceros as tall as a giraffe and as heavy as a bus. Its head alone was longer than your outstretched arms! Like a giraffe, it probably ate twigs and leaves from trees. It may even have had a short trunk.

This was truly the age of the rhinoceros!

THE END OF A NOBLE LINE

During the Oligocene, around 25 million years ago, rhinos were found across the world—from the massive *Paraceratherium* to its various smaller relatives. However, after this period the whole group went into a bit of a decline. Their place on the plains was taken by other beasts. Those rhino species that were left settled down into the familiar shape that we know today. But then, about 1.8 million years ago, the Ice Age arrived, and they once more had to adapt to a change in environment.

COELODONTA

Pronounced: See-loh-don-ta
Lived: 3.7 MYA–10,000 years ago
(Pliocene to Pleistocene)
Size: 12 ½ feet (3.8 m) long, without horn

Some rhino species adapted to colder conditions by growing shaggy hair for insulation. The most famous example is *Coelodonta*, the woolly rhinoceros, which ranged through Europe and Asia.

ELASMOTHERIUM

Pronounced: Eh-laz-moh-theer-ee-um
Lived: 2.6 MYA–28,000 years ago
(Pliocene to Pleistocene)
Size: 16 ½ feet (5 m) long, without horn

Elasmotherium also lived in Europe and Asia. It was very similar to *Coelodonta*, but its horn was truly enormous!

HOW DO WE KNOW?

For many extinct animals, all we have left is fossilized bones. Even those remains can't tell the whole story. For example, *Elasmotherium*'s huge horn was made of compacted hair, not bone. Hair rots away over time, so we have never found the remains of its horn. Our only evidence is the massive anchor space on top of the skull. But for other species, like *Coelodonta*, we are lucky enough to have eyewitness reports! There are pictures of it painted on cave walls by our own ancestors.

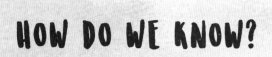

Odd toes

Rhinos are part of a line that we call the perissodactyls, which goes all the way back to *Hyrachyus*. These animals had an odd number of toes. Only five species of rhinoceros survive today, in small populations in parts of Africa and Asia. These rhinos are critically endangered. But another branch of perissodactyls survives in huge numbers across the world: the horse.

When it comes to evolution, both rhinos and horses have followed a common pattern. Their ancestors started out as small animals that could survive in a range of different habitats. Over generations, they split into different groups, each adapted to a particular habitat or lifestyle. Then some of the species began to die out. The few survivors are very specialized, meaning they are only able to thrive in one particular environment.

EOHIPPUS (sometimes called Hyracotherium)

Pronounced: Ee-oh-hip-us
Lived: 55–45 MYA (Eocene)
Size: 39 inches (1 m) long

Modern horses trace their ancestry to small, scampering forest browsers like *Eohippus*, which lived in North America and Europe. It had low-crowned teeth for eating leaves, and an odd number of toes: three on the back feet and five on the front, though one of those toes had almost completely disappeared.

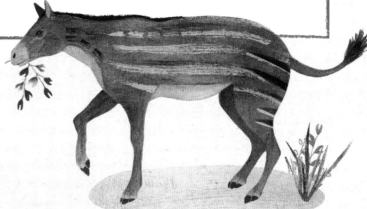

EQUUS (modern horse)

Pronounced: Eh-kwuss
Lives: present day
Size: 6 ½ feet (2 m) long

45 million years later, after all sorts of branches and sidelines, we have the single surviving horse genus: *Equus*. These graceful, running animals have a single toe on each foot. Their tall teeth are driven by powerful jaw muscles to tackle the tough grasses of the plains.

Successful relatives

Millions of years ago, perissodactyls (including the ancestors of rhinos and horses) ruled the plains. But they peaked early, and now it is their distant relatives, the artiodactyls, which are thriving. Artiodactyls have an even number of toes. The species that are still going strong today include camels, cows, sheep, deer, giraffes, and many more.

WHEN ELEPHANTS WERE TINY

What do you think of when you picture an elephant? A huge, solid body? A long, bendy trunk? Well, once upon a time, the elephant's ancestors were nothing like this!

Earliest elephants

A plump animal—about the size of a pig—stands on its four stumpy legs, wallowing in the shallow water of a tropical swamp. What is it? It looks a bit like a small hippopotamus, but it is *Moeritherium*—the earliest elephant that we know from complete remains. There was an earlier species, *Phosphatherium*, but scientists have only found parts of its skull. *Phosphatherium* had no sign of a trunk and its teeth suggest that it ate all kinds of things. The whole animal would have been less than 12 inches (30 centimeters) high at the shoulders.

MOERITHERIUM

Pronounced: Moh-reh-theer-ee-um
Lived: 37 MYA (Eocene)
Size: 8 feet (2.5 m) long

Like *Phosphatherium*, *Moeritherium* lived in North Africa. It may look a lot different from the modern elephant, but it bears a certain resemblance to the modern elephant's closest living relative—a cute little rabbit-sized animal called a hyrax.

Bigger bodies

From these humble beginnings, the standard elephant shape evolved pretty quickly. Within a few million years *Palaeomastodon* appeared, also in North Africa. It looked much more like the elephants we see today.

PALAEOMASTODON

Pronounced: Pay-lee-oh-mass-toh-don
Lived: 30 MYA (Oligocene)
Size: 7 feet (2.2 m) long

Palaeomastodon was large enough that its mouth was a long way from the ground, so it used its trunk to reach for food.

Large, heavy body

Short trunk and tusks

Strong, pillar-like legs

TREMENDOUS TUSKS

The trunk wasn't the only new development. Elephants' front teeth soon evolved into tusks, which helped the animals gather food. Throughout the rest of the Palaeogene period, there were many different tusk and trunk shapes. Here are just a few of them.

GOMPHOTHERIUM

Gomphotherium roamed across North America, Europe, Africa, and Asia up until about 3 million years ago. It had four tusks—two on the top jaw and two on the lower jaw.

DEINOTHERIUM

Tusks that curved downward were useful as picks for digging up roots and bulbs. *Deinotherium* had two downward-curving tusks on the lower jaw.

PLATYBELODON

Platybelodon was a shovel-tusker—the spade-shaped tusks in its lower jaw could scoop up soft water plants, or scrape twigs and bark from trees. Its broad trunk would drag food over the lower tusks and into the mouth, like a prehistoric vegetable grater.

ANANCUS

Anancus had the longest tusks of all the elephant species, at about 13 feet (4 meters) long. They took its total body length to a whopping 23 feet (7 meters)!

CUVIERONIUS

Cuvieronius was slightly smaller than *Anancus*, but it still had an impressive set of tusks, which had an unusual twisted shape.

Bigger and better

Elephants reached their large size for protection. Other animals protect themselves from enemies in different ways—by running away, by hiding, by using armor. The sheer size of an elephant keeps it safe from hunting animals.

Scientists have discovered that elephants evolved to their huge size in about 24 million generations, and most of this increase took place over about 25 million years, between the early Paleocene and late Eocene. During this time, elephants spread across the Americas, Europe, and Asia—all the continents, in fact, except Australia and Antarctica.

TOWARD THE MODERN ELEPHANTS

When the Ice Age came, about 1.8 million years ago, the temperature dropped. Many animals had to adapt to survive the new conditions, including the elephants. Their sheer size was a good start. Their big bodies were good at keeping in heat, helping them to cope with lower temperatures.

Several types of elephant also evolved hairy coats to provide extra insulation. The two most famous of these were the mastodon and the mammoth. But don't let the hair fool you—they were quite different animals. The main difference was in their teeth.

MAMMUT

Pronounced: Ma-mut
Lived: 20 MYA–10,000 years ago
(Miocene to Pleistocene)
Size: 20 feet (6 m) long, including tusks

Mammut sounds like it should be the mammoth, but it's actually the proper name for the mastodon! It had teeth with a grinding surface of rounded cones. It ranged across North America, Africa, Europe, and Asia.

MAMMUTHUS

Pronounced: Ma-moo-thuss
Lived: 5 MYA–5,000 years ago
(Pliocene to modern times)
Size: 20 feet (6 m) long, including tusks

Also living across North America, Europe, and Asia, *Mammuthus*, the mammoth, had teeth covered in ridges. They look much more like the teeth of the modern elephant. There are eyewitness reports of what the mammoth looked like, drawn and engraved on cave walls throughout Europe.

A ginger elephant?

The woolly mammoth is often shown covered in red hair, but this may be wrong. Scientists often find mammoth remains preserved in frozen soil, with their skin and hair intact. The hair is usually a reddish color. However, scientists think that the hair was originally straw-colored, and only turned red after death.

The giants shrink again

During the Ice Age, a huge amount of water was frozen in glaciers and ice caps. There was so much ice that its weight pushed the northern continents downward! These changes meant that sea levels also changed. Some animals were trapped on islands and had to adapt to island life.

On the island of Malta in the Mediterranean there was a population of elephants. Over time, these became much smaller, to cope with the limited amount of food available on the island.

There was even a dwarf mammoth on the Channel Islands off California in the USA!

MODERN ELEPHANTS

Now there are only two groups of modern elephants—the African and the Asian. The African elephant has become particularly well adapted to a warmer climate. It has replaced insulating fur with wrinkly skin that helps to let out body heat, and its huge ears act like radiators, releasing body heat as they flap about in the wind.

WHEN BIRDS STOPPED FLYING

Some birds just don't fly. Despite all the evolutionary changes made during the time of the dinosaurs—changes that made birds the ideal flying animals—some bird lines gave up the power of flight and became land-living animals. We call this bird group the ratites.

The only modern ratites are the ostrich, emu, rhea, cassowary, and kiwi. Ostriches have wings with big feathers used only for display, while kiwis have hardly any trace of wing bones at all. Although the ostrich is the largest living bird, recently extinct ratites were much bigger. If we look even further back, to the Palaeogene period (66–23 million years ago), some weren't just big—they were truly monstrous!

DINORNIS

Pronounced: Dih-nor-niss
Lived: 1.45 MYA to 600 years ago
   (Pliocene to modern times)
Size: 12 feet (3.6 m) tall

Commonly called the giant moa, this bird lived in New Zealand and was hunted by the islands' first settlers. There were half a dozen species, the smallest of which was about turkey-sized.

AEPYORNIS

Pronounced: Ee-pee-or-niss
Lived: 2 MYA to 1,000 years ago
   (Pliocene to modern times)
Size: 10 feet (3 m) tall

Also known as the elephant bird, this species was native to Madagascar and weighed as much as 880 pounds (400 kg). It only became extinct 1,000 years ago, so its existence may have led to folk legends of giant birds such as the Roc.

Why did giant, flightless birds evolve?

At the beginning of the Palaeogene period, the ratites thrived. Dinosaurs had gone extinct and the big hunting mammals had not yet evolved. Without the need to take flight to escape predators, the ratites were able to grow bigger and heavier. Some fierce flightless birds even became the big predators of their time.

Millions of years later, as hunting mammals took over, the ratites became restricted to islands and island continents where there were no other big predators. There were no lions on Madagascar, and so *Aepyornis* survived. There were no wolves in New Zealand, and so the kiwis and moas thrived...until humans arrived, at least.

GASTORNIS

Pronounced: Gas-tor-niss
Lived: 50 MYA (Late Paleocene
    to Early Eocene)
Size: 6 ½ feet (2 m) tall

Despite its fearsome appearance,
Gastornis was probably
a plant-eater, using its
huge beak to rip up
tough vegetation.

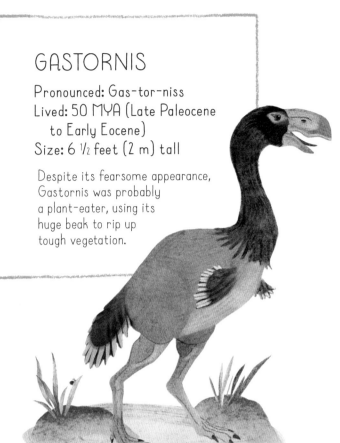

KELENKEN

Pronounced: Kell-en-ken
Lived: 15 MYA (Miocene)
Size: 10 feet (3 m) tall

This giant predator had tiny clawed
wings, just like the forelimbs of that
other fierce killer, *Tyrannosaurus rex.*

WHERE DID THEY COME FROM?

Scientists used to think that ratites evolved when all the
continents were a single landmass, and that when this landmass
broke up into different continents the ratites went with
them. That would explain why ostriches live in Africa, rheas
in South America, and emus in Australia.

Now we think it more likely that they evolved on each
continent from separate ancestors that were able to
fly there. A possible ancestor of the modern New
Zealand kiwi is tiny *Proapteryx.* It may have flown to
New Zealand from Australia, where the kiwi's nearest
relatives—the cassowary and emu—live to this day.

Proapteryx

Modern kiwi

As far as we know, no flightless bird
has ever regained the ability to fly.

WHEN MAMMALS BEGAN TO HUNT

When you picture a top predator today, you might think of a prowling lion or a pack of wolves. In fact, the family of mammals that includes cats and dogs, known as Carnivora, were late starters. They didn't become the dominant meat-eating animals until well into the Palaeogene period. This period is sometimes called the Age of Mammals.

At the beginning of the Palaeogene, just after the dinosaurs died out, giant, flightless birds were the main meat-eaters. But gradually, over millions of years, hunting mammals appeared. A primitive group called the creodonts were the first to emerge. They came in all shapes and sizes, depending on the prey they hunted.

TRITEMNODON

Pronounced: Try-tem-no-don
Lived: 50 MYA (Eocene)
Size: 4 feet (1.5 m) long, including its long tail

Tritemnodon was shaped a bit like a mongoose. Hunting on the ground and in trees in North America, it preyed upon all sorts of small animals.

HYAENODON

Pronounced: Hi-ee-noh-don
Lived: 23 MYA (Miocene)
Size: 1 ½–10 feet (0.5–3 m) long

Hyaenodon was about the size of a wolf and hunted animals bigger than itself. It lived throughout North America, Africa, Europe, and Asia.

MEGISTOTHERIUM

Pronounced: Meg-isto-theer-ee-um
Lived: 23 MYA (Miocene)
Size: 10 feet (3 m) long

Megistotherium had a huge head and was bigger than a bear. Native to Africa, it was probably the biggest meat-eating land mammal that ever lived.

All change

During the time that the fierce creodonts ruled, another group of smaller animals kept well out of their way. These were the Carnivora, or "true carnivores". The earliest true carnivores were weasel-sized animals like *Miacis*. When the creodonts died out, the true carnivores took over. Scientists are still not sure why. Perhaps it was because the creodonts' brains were much smaller, or perhaps because their limbs were not as versatile.

As soon as they began to flourish, the true carnivores split into two separate groups. One was made up of cats, hyenas, and mongooses. The other contained the dogs, bears, seals, and weasels. We're going to take a closer look at the group that evolved into cats.

MIACIS

Pronounced: My-ah-sis
Lived: 55 MYA (Paleocene)
Size: 12 inches (30 cm) long

Miacis is thought to be one of the earliest carnivores that lived in trees, where it hunted smaller animals. It is the ancestor of modern dogs, wolves, foxes, coyotes, bears, raccoons, and weasels.

Proailurus had a much longer head than any modern cat.

PROAILURUS

Pronounced: Pro-eye-lur-us
Lived: 20 MYA (Miocene)
Size: 24 inches (60 cm) long

Living in Europe and Asia, *Proailurus* was built a bit like a modern marten. It also resembled the earlier creodont *Tritemnodon*, although they weren't closely related. Like a marten, it spent much of its time hunting in trees.

HOPLOPHONEUS

Pronounced: Hop-loh-fon-ee-us
Lived: 30 MYA (Oligocene)
Size: 4 feet (1.2 m) long

By the time that North American *Hoplophoneus* came along, the familiar shape of the cat had evolved. This was a sneaky animal that could hide, creep up on its prey, and pounce. Its ferocious teeth were meant for killing—something that the cats went on to do best.

Stealthy cats

The toes of *Hoplophoneus* incorporated a unique joint. It enabled the claws to be lifted off the ground out of the way, and only brought out when needed. The dog family never developed this and so their claws are always in contact with the ground. That is why a dog goes clickety-clickety-clickety when it runs along the road, whereas you never hear a cat approach!

MY, WHAT BIG TEETH!

Many of the cats that evolved during the Palaeogene had to kill prey much larger than themselves. To do this, several different branches of the family (shown below) evolved huge canine teeth—much bigger than the teeth of modern cats.

Dirk-toothed cats

Megantereon had large upper canine teeth. When the mouth was closed, they fitted neatly and safely alongside bony outgrowths of the lower jaw, but when the mouth was open they became fearsome weapons. This cat probably hunted by ambush, like a modern leopard. It could bring down the horses of the time, holding on with its strong front legs and slashing at the throat with its big teeth.

Scimitar-toothed cats

Homotherium had even longer canines, with serrated edges like a steak knife. These were great for slicing the meat off animals which had already been killed. *Homotherium* and other scimitar-toothed cats had long front legs but shorter hind legs. They lived in colder climates and probably hunted by running down young mammoths.

Saber-toothed cats

The biggest teeth of all belonged to the saber-toothed cats, like *Smilodon*. At 8 feet (2.5 meters) long, these cats were much bigger than any modern cat. They could open their mouths at a gape of 120 degrees. This allowed the 12-inch (30-centimeter)-long teeth to drive downward, powered by huge neck muscles to deliver a ferocious killing blow.

When is a cat not a cat?

The saber-toothed pattern was such a good adaptation that it evolved totally independently in South America. Although *Thylacosmilus* (7–4 million years ago) looked like a saber-toothed cat, it was actually a marsupial, and related to modern kangaroos!

Biters, not slashers

There are no saber-toothed cats alive today. And not all prehistoric cats had those huge teeth, either. Another important group was called the "biting cats" rather than the "slashing cats." Even without saber teeth, they were still pretty fearsome—the cave lion, the biggest cat of all, weighed up to 770 pounds (350 kilograms)! This is the group whose members still survive to this day.

Flexible, spring-like backbone gives extra power for sprinting.

Short face with big nostrils for taking in plenty of air.

Long, heavy tail provides balance.

Long legs for running.

MIRACINONYX

Pronounced: Mi-rah-sin-on-ix
Lived: 2 MYA–10,000 years ago (Pleistocene)
Size: 4 feet (1.5 m long), without tail

Just like a modern cheetah, *Miracinonyx* was built for speed. It lived on the prairies of North America, where it chased swift-footed grazers like pronghorns.

PANTHERA LEO SPELAEA

Pronounced: Pan-ther-ah lee-oh spell-ee-ah
Lived: 600,000–30,000 years ago (Pleistocene)
Size: 7 feet (2.1 m) long, without tail

The cave lion was a close relative of the modern lion, but at least ten percent bigger. It hunted mammoths and reindeer at the height of the Ice Age, all the way from Europe, across Asia and Alaska. Our ancestors must have come face to face with these terrifying beasts—they painted them on their cave walls.

WHEN PRIMATES CAME DOWN FROM THE TREES

Have you ever visited a zoo or a wildlife park and found yourself enchanted by the cute, big-eyed lemurs, or amazed at the South American monkeys dangling by their strong tails? Maybe you've admired the apes as they swing from the branches, hanging by their big hands. We are fascinated by this group of animals because they are our closest relatives. They are the primates—the mammal family to which humans belong.

Mysterious origins

Scientists can tell from the DNA of modern species that the first primates must have emerged way back during the Cretaceous period. So far, no one has found any primate fossils dating back that far, but there are plenty of remains from the beginning of the Palaeogene, 65 million years ago.

The first primates would have been difficult to tell apart from the other early mammals of the time. The earliest ones were tiny and probably looked a bit like the modern tree shrew. Primates this small would not have been able to eat enough leaves to get the nourishment they needed. They must have eaten insects, which pack in more nutrients.

The very earliest primates probably looked like this.

Eyes on the side of the head, more like a rodent than a modern primate.

Small teeth suitable for catching and eating insects.

A tail to help with balance

Short toes and claws for climbing around in the trees, like a squirrel.

PLESIADAPIS

Pronounced: Plee-zee-ah-day-piss
Lived: 60 MYA (Palaeocene)
Size: 32 inches (80 cm) long

Scientists used to think that
Plesiadapis, which lived in North
America and Europe, was an early
primate. We now know that it was a
different type of mammal. However,
the primates of this time, which are
mostly known only from their fossil
teeth, would probably have looked very
much like *Plesiadapis*.

Branching out

Once the primates as a group evolved, they
quickly branched out into different lines.
One was a group we call the prosimians.
Their modern descendants are the lemurs
that now roam Madagascar.

Bigger brains

The other line of primates became
the monkeys. Like early primates
and prosimians, the monkeys also
lived in trees. What set them apart
was that they began to develop
bigger brains. A big brain has many
advantages, but the downside is
that it uses a lot of energy. In fact,
the human brain uses 25 percent of
a person's total energy intake!

NANNOPITHEX

Pronounced: Nah-no-pih-thex
Lived: 50 MYA (Palaeocene)
Size: 16 inches (40 cm) long

Nannopithex was an early
form of prosimian, found in
what is now Europe. It looked
a bit like the modern tarsier.

AEGYPTOPITHECUS

Pronounced: Ee-jip-toh-pith-eh-kuss
Lived: 30 MYA (Oligocene)
Size: 22-36 inches (56-92 cm) long

One of the earliest true monkeys
that we know is *Aegyptopithecus*,
from Egypt. Most early primates
are only known from teeth, but for
Aegyptopithecus we have skull
parts and limb bones as well.

So why did monkeys need bigger brains? There are several possible
reasons. One is that as they began to eat fruit, they had to be
able to tell edible and poisonous fruits apart. Another is that
living in trees is dangerous—one slip and it is a long way down! The
skill and concentration needed to stay safe would require more
brainpower. In addition, monkeys lived in groups, so they needed
the ability to interact with one another and pass on knowledge.

Once monkeys had evolved, what came next?

TWO KINDS OF MONKEY

In time, the monkey line itself split into two. One group was the platyrrhines—the flat-nosed monkeys. These are the monkeys that we find in South America today, using their strong prehensile tails to swing through the trees. The other group was the catarrhines—the narrow-nosed monkeys. They developed and spread in Africa and Asia. Unlike the platyrrhines, their tails cannot grasp.

PERUPITHECUS

Pronounced: Per-oo-pith-eh-kuss
Lived: 36 MYA (Eocene)
Size: 24 inches (60 cm) long

Perupithecus was an early example of a platyrrhine from South America. Although it lived during the Eocene, it looked very much like the modern monkeys which live in the same area today.

SAADANIUS

Pronounced: Saa-day-ni-us
Lived: 28 MYA (Oligocene)
Size: 39 inches (1 m) tall

Saadanius, from Arabia, was an early example of a catarrhine. It walked in the branches of trees, very much like the modern langur. However, it had a longer snout.

PROSIMIANS   MONKEYS   APES

Lemurs   Lorises   Tarsiers   New world monkeys   Old world monkeys   Gibbons   Orangutans   Gorillas   Chimpanzees   Humans

Ancestral primate

This cladogram shows the relationship between the different branches of the primate family, and how closely or distantly related each is to the others.

RISE OF THE APES

Some time after the catarrhine monkeys established themselves in Africa and Asia, the climate changed, along with the landscape. Evolution means that when this happens, changes in an animal's body and behavior that help it survive the new conditions will be passed on to the next generation. This is how a side branch of the catarrhine family split off and became the apes. We can tell apes apart from their ancestors by the lack of a tail, the ability to live both in trees and on the ground, and their larger brains.

Gibbons, orangutans, gorillas, chimpanzees, and bonobos are modern apes. The earliest ancestor that we know of is *Nakalipithecus*, which lived in Kenya about 10 million years ago. The only remains that have been found are jawbones and teeth. As for the rest of the body, we don't know what it looked like! It might have walked on all fours, like a baboon, or on its hind legs.

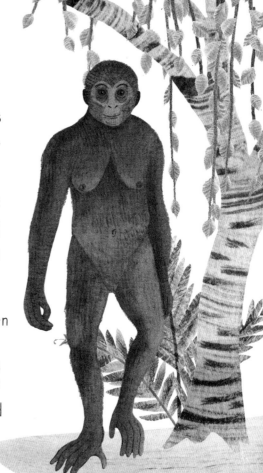

From the trees to the ground

Oreopithecus was an ape that appeared in Italy about a million years later. It could walk on its hind legs, but it was more at home in the trees, with feet and swinging arms like a chimpanzee. Its broad shoulders and short body show that it was a tree-swinger, and was not yet fully adapted to walking on the ground.

ORRORIN

Pronounced: Or-ror-in
Lived: 6 MYA (Miocene)
Size: 4 feet (1.2 m) tall

Orrorin's legs were attached to its hips in a way that provided a strong support for walking on two feet.

GIANTS AMONG US

The biggest primate that we know was *Gigantopithecus*, which roamed parts of Asia from 9 million years ago. This enormous ape was built like a modern gorilla, but at 10 feet (3 meters) tall, it was twice the size! Its descendants were alive at the same time as early humans.

OUR PART IN THE STORY

Toward the end of the Pliocene, Earth's climate was changing, beginning its long cooling toward the Pleistocene Ice Age. This brought changing environments, including forest areas turning to grassland and savanna. A new line of primate evolved from part of the ape group.

These new primates were better adapted to the new open conditions. They walked on two legs, and so were no longer reliant on living in trees. They were tall and stood upright, so they could look over high grass. As they no longer needed to grasp branches, their hands were free to be used in other tasks. These primates were not covered in fur, which meant they did not overheat on the open plains. The ancestors of modern people had appeared.

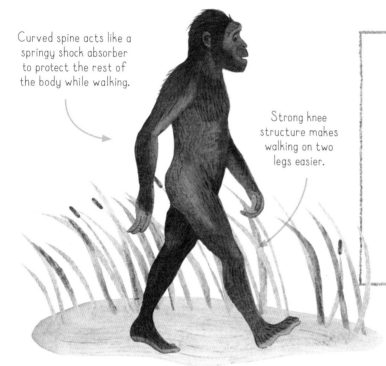

Curved spine acts like a springy shock absorber to protect the rest of the body while walking.

Strong knee structure makes walking on two legs easier.

AUSTRALOPITHECUS

Pronounced: Ost-ra-lo-pith-eh-kuss
Lived: 2.5 MYA (Pliocene)
Where: East Africa
Size: 4 ½ feet (1.4 m) tall

By the time that *Australopithecus* emerged, about 4 million years ago, walking was the main mode of locomotion.

Humans at last!

Just before the beginning of the Ice Age, a group of related species known as *Homo* appeared in east Africa. At first there were several species, including *Homo ergaster* and *Homo habilis*—the latter being the first that we know who made tools. From these, the only survivor was *Homo erectus*, who then spread to Europe and Asia, and from which evolved modern humans.

HOMO HABILIS

Pronounced: Ho-mo ha-bill-iss
Lived: 2.4–1.4 MYA (Pleistocene)
Where: Sub-Saharan Africa
Size: 39–53 inches (1–1.35 m) tall

Homo habilis means "handy man." It was given this name because it was the first to make and use primitive stone tools. These were merely sharp flakes of stone which may have been used to scrape meat off bones.

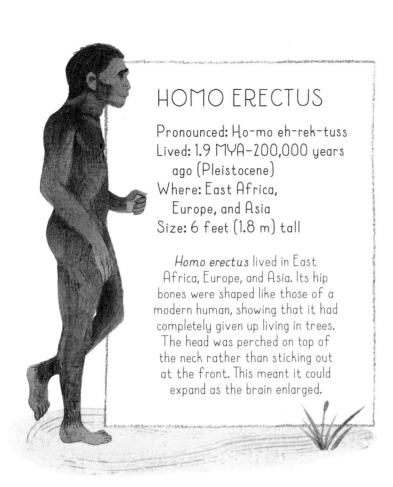

HOMO ERECTUS

Pronounced: Ho-mo eh-rek-tuss
Lived: 1.9 MYA–200,000 years
ago (Pleistocene)
Where: East Africa,
Europe, and Asia
Size: 6 feet (1.8 m) tall

Homo erectus lived in East
Africa, Europe, and Asia. Its hip
bones were shaped like those of a
modern human, showing that it had
completely given up living in trees.
The head was perched on top of
the neck rather than sticking out
at the front. This meant it could
expand as the brain enlarged.

A SMALL HUMAN

From about 74,000
to 17,000 years ago,
there was a very small
human living on the
islands of Indonesia—
Homo floresiensis.
They were only around
43 inches tall! Dwarf
forms on islands are
fairly common. The
food supply is often
limited, so a smaller
size means less
food is needed.

HOMO SAPIENS

Pronounced: Ho-mo sah-pi-ens
Lives: 300,000 years ago–present day
Where: originated in Africa, now worldwide

Homo sapiens, whose name means "wise man," has
a larger brain size than earlier humans. There are
certain differences between groups of *Homo sapiens*—
different eye color, skin color and hair color, and
variations in height and build—but they are
all recognizable as a single species.

Many human species

Not so long ago, there were several species of humans living at the same time. More species of *Homo*
evolved from *Homo erectus*, including *Homo neanderthalensis* (Neanderthal Man) in Europe, which died
out only 40,000 years ago, *Homo rhodesiensis* and *Homo sapiens* in Africa and *Homo heidelbergensis*
in Africa, Europe, and Asia. Scientists are still arguing about the relationships of these, but one thing is
clear—*Homo sapiens* was the only one to survive until the present day. Ourselves!

EVOLUTION CONTINUES

Reading a book like this might give you the impression that we know all about the history of life on our planet. In fact, we don't! Just look how uncertain we are when it comes to our own recent ancestors. There is still so much that we do not know—so much we have yet to find out.

This is what makes the study of ancient animals and of evolution so exciting. Every year, new discoveries are made. These discoveries might be fossils of animals that haven't been seen before, or they can be genetic breakthroughs in the study of today's animals, which tell us more about their history.

But evolution is not something that happened in the past, got us where we are today, and then stopped. Rather, it is a continuous process. Animals are going extinct all the time, and when they do, their places will eventually be taken by something else, evolving from what has survived. Evolution is such a slow process that we may not see it working, but it continues regardless.

Are we experiencing a mass extinction?

There have been about half a dozen times in Earth's history when huge numbers of species have died out. These events are called mass extinctions. In many ways, mass extinctions provide a huge boost to evolution. They allow the animals that are left to exploit new environments, through the processes of mutation and natural selection. For example, the mass extinction at the end of the Cretaceous period wiped out the dinosaurs, but it was the beginning of the age of mammals—leading eventually to modern humans.

We are currently in the middle of another mass extinction. But instead of being caused by asteroid impacts or volcanic activity, this one is caused by humans. Our global, connected world means that animals and plants can easily spread from one continent to another, where they take over new areas, forcing out the former occupants. Over-hunting and over-fishing have wiped out some species. Burning fossil fuels causes climate change, which can drastically change habitats. Animals that can adapt to the new conditions may survive, but those that can't will die out.

What of the future?

In the far future, the Earth will change. There are changes that we can predict, such as the movement of continents. The Atlantic ocean will continue to widen, Australia will continue to move northward, East Africa will split off along the Great Rift Valley, and the Mediterranean Sea will vanish and scrunch up into a mountain range.

Then there are changes that we cannot predict. Another ice age? A meteorite impact? One thing we can be sure of—life will survive and adapt. It will go on and continue to evolve for as long as the Earth exists. And that will be a long, long time.

INDEX